More Praise for *Baking with Steel*

"Every decade or two, a revolutionary idea turns into a revolutionary product that actually does change the way we make our food. . . . This book distills the passion and dedication of Andris Lagsdin and Jessie Oleson Moore into a series of recipes and techniques that will help you make some of the best pizza, steak, and pancakes and show you how a simple slab of steel can fundamentally change the way you feed your family."

—from the foreword by **J. Kenji López-Alt,** bestselling author of *The Food Lab* and managing culinary director of Serious Eats

"The Baking Steel has revolutionized how pizza should be made at home. After baking on a Steel in my own kitchen, I can't see any home cook not needing one—or even two—for baking, pizza making, and much, much more. It's the only way I know to make pizzeria-quality pizza in your home oven, and *Baking with Steel* gives you all the tools to unlock the Steel's full potential in your kitchen."

—**Tony Gemignani,** master instructor at the International School of Pizza and author of *The Pizza Bible*

"My Baking Steel never leaves the oven. I love the crust it creates on everything I bake; not just pizza, but bread and pie too! The results are fantastic, and I no longer worry about cracked baking stones. It's brilliant!" —**Zoë François,** author of *Artisan Bread in Five Minutes a Day*

"Andris Lagsdin changed the game by creating the Baking Steel, and he developed a range of delicious recipes to use it to transform every course, from breakfast to dessert. *Baking with Steel* shows you how to do it all." —**Alex Talbot,** coauthor of *Ideas in Food*

"The Baking Steel is an essential tool for the avid cook. With this book and a Steel in your oven, you too will make perfect, professional-quality breads, pizza, and more at home."

—**Jenn Louis,** chef and author of *Pasta by Hand* and *The Book of Greens*

"*Baking with Steel* displays Andris Lagsdin's unique mastery of both steel and the art of pizza. The Baking Steel is an incredible kitchen tool you'll use all year round, and this book is the perfect companion for your culinary adventures."

—**Ming Tsai,** chef and author of *Simply Ming*

BAKING with STEEL

BAKING *with* STEEL

The Revolutionary New Approach to
Perfect Pizza, Bread, and More

Andris Lagsdin
with Jessie Oleson Moore

Foreword by J. Kenji López-Alt

VORACIOUS
LITTLE, BROWN AND COMPANY
New York Boston London

Voracious / Little, Brown and Company
Hachette Book Group
1290 Avenue of the Americas, New York, NY 10104
littlebrown.com

First Edition: December 2017

Voracious is an imprint of Little, Brown and Company, a division of Hachette Book Group, Inc. The Voracious name and logo are trademarks of Hachette Book Group, Inc.

The publisher is not responsible for websites (or their content) that are not owned by the publisher.

Interior photography by Andris Lagsdin
Interior design by Gary Tooth / Empire Design Studio

ISBN 978-0-316-46578-6
LCCN 2017939505

10 9 8 7 6 5 4 3

1010

Printed in China

CONTENTS

FOREWORD

by J. Kenji López-Alt

It's rare to see a truly new kitchen product in the food world. Sure, there are dozens of TV infomercials hawking revolutionary new blenders or countertop rotisseries that'll change your life, but really they're all the same old crap with a new coat of paint.

But every decade or two, a revolutionary idea turns into a revolutionary product that actually does change the way we make our food. The pressure cooker in the 1930s. The microwave oven in the 1950s. Sous-vide ovens in the late 1970s. In 2012, when I first reached out to Andris Lagsdin about giving his new Baking Steel a spin, I never suspected that it would make the list. I mean, come on. It's just a plain old slab of steel. How revolutionary could it be?

Well, if you've ever tried to make great pizza in a home oven, the answer is *very*.

You see, in order to make pizza—and I mean great pizza—you need to cook it hot. Wood-fired Neapolitan pizza ovens hit floor and dome temperatures in excess of 900 degrees, while New York–style pizza ovens regularly bake at 600 to 700 degrees. It's this extreme heat that converts a disk of raw dough into a perfect pizza crust, one that crackles as you bite into it but gives way to a moist, cloudlike, lightly stretchy interior crumb. Use that same dough in a home oven—even one with a baking stone— and it cooks too slowly. By the time it crisps up, it's dried out to a cracker-like finish.

A home oven simply doesn't get hot enough to cook really great pizza.

At least, that's what I'd always thought. Turns out the most important thing isn't temperature—it's energy. The faster you transfer heat energy into baking pizza dough, the faster it cooks. Enter the Baking Steel. Compared to a baking stone, the Baking Steel has higher conductivity (meaning that it transfers heat energy faster) and a higher volumetric heat capacity (meaning that it can store more heat energy per cubic inch), so it doesn't have to cook hotter.

You're probably already familiar with this phenomenon. Everyone's gotten burned by boiling water (which is 212 degrees Fahrenheit); it happens almost instantly. But you can easily reach into a 500-degree oven and hold your hand there for several seconds without much discomfort. Water conducts heat better than air, and the same principle applies to steel and stone.

Even at the exact same oven temperature, steel can pump energy into pizza dough several times faster than stone can. Equipped with a Baking Steel, not only did I make the best pizza I'd ever made in a home oven, but I did it in record time. Pizzas that took ten to twelve minutes to cook on a baking stone baked up in four minutes with puffy, crisp, moist crusts on the Baking Steel. Instead of an every-few-months thing, pizza became a once-a-week thing. Even store-bought pizza dough goes from passable to incredible when baked on steel.

I didn't know Andris before I found out about the Baking Steel, but I've gotten to know him quite well since then. I'm impressed by his passion for tinkering with and improving on this seemingly simple product and by his openness to new ideas and direction. For example, early on I mentioned to Andris that I'd tried throwing the Baking Steel on my stovetop to cook some eggs, using it as a sort of makeshift griddle. A few months later I was looking at the shiny, polished surface of the Baking Steel Griddle, milled grease channel and all.

The mini version of that griddle now has a permanent home over one of my burners. I use its massive thermal capacity and nonstick surface (it seasons up just like a cast-iron pan) to cook batches of perfectly browned pancakes and French toast. I crisp up bacon and fry my toast in the drippings; I get it smoking hot and blacken shrimp right in their shells before giving them a drizzle of olive oil and a squeeze of lemon juice. I make smashed hamburgers with crispy edges and deeply browned flavor, and I can sear steaks faster than I've ever seared them.

This book distills the passion and dedication of Andris Lagsdin and Jessie Oleson Moore—another friend and colleague of mine—into a series of recipes and techniques that will help you make some of the best pizza, steak, and pancakes you've ever made and show you how a simple slab of steel can fundamentally change the way you feed your family.

BAKING WITH
STEEL

INTRODUCTION
The Story of Steel

The two things in life I know best are steel and pizza.

My dad's a steel man. My brother's a steel man. And I suppose somewhere deep inside, I'm a steel man too. My family owns the Stoughton Steel Company in the South Shore of Boston, where we've made industrial steel products for over forty years.

But when I was young, I didn't want much to do with the family business. I left to see the world; I became a tennis instructor and held every service job imaginable. Along the way I learned that I loved working in restaurant kitchens. There's something about the energy, the hustle, and, of course, the food.

In my twenties I landed a job in Boston slinging pizza at Figs, celebrated chef Todd English's restaurant. Todd was at the leading edge of the artisanal-pizza movement; he sourced local ingredients and championed the now-trendy, airy thin-crust pizza long before anyone used the phrase *farm to table*. My time at Figs gave me an education that I couldn't have gotten anywhere else.

I already liked pizza, but after working for Todd, I lived for it. There's the quiet, meditative task of prepping: the feel of dough in your hands, the comforting repetition of chopping and stirring. There's the sweet aroma of rising dough and the acidic zing of fresh tomato sauce. And the most fulfilling part of making pizza is the sense of connection and creativity that comes with the process. It's even better when it's a family, friend, or party activity.

But although homemade pizza is fun to make, the pie never quite measures up to the kind with the perfectly crisp crust you get straight out of a restaurant's screaming-hot brick oven. For years, I—and every serious home cook I knew—used a baking stone to make pizza in the kitchen oven, assuming it was the best way to approximate the charred, blistered pizza-oven crusts. Even with my training, though, I couldn't make restaurant-quality pizza that way.

I transitioned from Todd's kitchen to his management team, but after a few years, I was burned out by the hectic pace and unforgiving hours. My dad asked if I'd come back to the family business, and I said yes. I gave it my all—but part of me dreamed about starting a new business, one related to food.

One day at work, I read an article in the *Wall Street Journal* about Nathan Myhrvold's *Modernist Cuisine*. In that hallowed encyclopedia of food science, the author made a keen observation about the physics of baking. He said, essentially, "The best conductor for creating a perfect pizza crust is not stone, but steel." If I were anyone else, I might have thought about it for a second, nodded, and then moved on with my life. But I'm not anyone else; I'm a steel man with a passion for pizza. This felt like fate.

I sprinted into the plant and hunted for the thinnest piece of metal available. I found a rusty scrap that had once been a Caterpillar part. It wasn't pretty, but it looked like just the right size for my experiment.

I brought it home and told my wife it was my new pizza stone, and she looked at me like I was crazy. But that first pizza I made was a revelation; it was done in half the time it took on my traditional pizza stone, and the perfect, airy crispness of the crust brought me back to the days of working with a 900-degree wood-fired oven. Encouraged by my first test, I cautiously mentioned my experiment to my brother and father, who ran Stoughton Steel, and gently suggested it could be a new product for us. Their reaction was...skeptical. The factory produced stabilizer pads for backhoes, not kitchenware. How on earth were a bunch of steel guys going to bring a home-pizza product to market?

I didn't trust my instincts, so I decided to shelve the project. Still, the idea stuck with me. I woke up every morning for six months thinking about the pizza steel. Then one day I found the confidence to take the leap and do everything I could to bring the product to life. I had been working hard for the past fifteen years, but I hadn't been pursuing my passion. I had two young boys, and I thought of the example I was setting for them. Sure, I was in a comfortable spot in my career, but comfort is not the same thing as fulfillment. I wanted to show them you can get up every day and do what you love.

I already knew the steel worked. I brought up my idea for a steel baking surface with my father and brother again, less cautiously now, and they began to come around. Perhaps it was my confidence in the product, or maybe they were convinced by the amazing pizzas I was making. I refined the prototype and they started to see how my passion project could become a source of income.

Launching a new product isn't as simple as putting an item in a box with a logo and shipping it out. In developing the steel, I had to consider its size, shape, and weight; what would work without being too cumbersome? I obsessively measured the temperatures and sizes of various ovens (probably making myself a person of interest at Home Depot in the process). I practically wore ruts in the pavement between our production facility and my parents' kitchen as I tried out each new version and developed a seasoning process to make the steel food-safe.

The more I tested the steel, the more versatile I realized it was. It could be used for roasting meat and vegetables and baking bread; it could even be frozen and used to make slab-style ice cream creations. But what would we call it? I have my brilliant wife to thank for the name: Baking Steel. It was perfect—like the product, the name was basic, simple, and about more than just pizza.

In the beginning, I was so focused on making the steel work that I didn't have any idea how many I might sell. Selling even one seemed like a good place to start. I'd seen other small businesses find success with crowdfunding platforms, and I decided that was what we needed to do to prove that the steel was a viable product. I set a modest goal on Kickstarter of three thousand dollars, just enough to cover the first production run.

I knew the Baking Steel made the best home-oven pizza I'd ever tasted, and I had the support of my friends and family, but would anyone else care? After all, nearly two-thirds of Kickstarter projects never get fully funded.

As soon as the site went live, I reached out to everyone I'd ever talked to, dated, or bought a latte from. A day later, we made our goal. It was really happening!

Before the campaign closed, something incredible happened. J. Kenji López-Alt, the managing culinary director of the popular food website Serious Eats, e-mailed to ask if he could try one out. A couple of days later he posted a review stating that the Baking Steel blew his favorite pizza stone out of the water. Things snowballed and the number of backers doubled.

Our first Baking Steel shipped in 2014. Since then, we've brought restaurant-quality baking projects to thousands of homes. I've opened a test kitchen near my Boston-area home, and I work with an amazing chef, Craig Hastings, to develop recipes. The Baking Steel has inspired a new generation of pizza makers. And with our new griddle-surface Baking Steel, we've brought the cooking power of steel to a wider range of foods. Baking Steel enthusiasts are always dreaming up new recipes, from whoopie pies to roasted vegetables to perfect steaks to, yes, even English muffins, and some of them kindly provided recipes for this book. (If you come up with a new Baking Steel recipe, share it with me at andris@bakingsteel.com.)

It's amazing what a piece of steel has done for my life. Let me show you what it can do in your kitchen.

1

BEFORE YOU BAKE

BEFORE YOU BAKE

Get the Most Out of Your Baking Steel

WHY IT WORKS

Why the Baking Steel? It's a valid question. It may be tempting to think of the Baking Steel as a novelty gadget for kitchen geeks. But this is far from a foodie fad. As this book will show you, the Baking Steel is a culinary powerhouse: a kitchen tool for chefs of all levels that can revolutionize the way you cook and bake.

Let's start out simple. Say you put a pizza on an aluminum baking sheet and put it in the oven. Your pizza will cook, but it will never attain the crispy crust that you'd get at a pizzeria. Without a superheated surface, you won't get the right balance of fully cooked toppings and crispy crust.

You might own a baking stone, which is a step in the right direction. A baking stone simulates the conditions of a commercial oven, but it's a poor substitute for it. That's not the case with the Baking Steel, which has a thermal conductivity eighteen times greater than a ceramic pizza stone's. The Baking Steel retains heat more evenly and for longer than a baking stone does, so it cooks pizzas faster and more effectively.

But perhaps the biggest advantage of the Baking Steel is that it has so many applications. The Baking Steel doesn't need to be relegated to the oven. It can be put on the stovetop—on both gas and electric burners—and used as a griddle or as a stand-in for a cast-iron skillet. It retains heat and allows for perfect griddling, stove-top cooking, and even searing. It can be placed directly on the grate of an outdoor grill or atop cans of Sterno to provide a hot surface on the fly. It can also be chilled, which means it's an invaluable tool for making pastry and confections and for serving and keeping cold dishes, well, cold.

The Baking Steel is also virtually indestructible. Many avid bakers have horror stories about their pizza stones shattering. With proper care, your steel will join you for a lifetime of culinary adventures. This unique yet simple slab of steel presents a whole new way to cook and bake. Enjoy the adventure.

BAKING STEEL 411

Every good chef knows that to get the most out of kitchen equipment, you must treat it with respect. The Baking Steel is built to last, but only if you take good care of it. Here's what you need to know.

YOUR FIRST TIME

The Baking Steel is pre-seasoned, so when you remove it from its packaging, it is ready for use. Wipe it off with a dry cloth, if you like, and remember to lift with your

Sometimes, the proof is in the pudding (or, in this case, the crust). Let's look at the differences in pizza crusts baked on various surfaces.

BAKING SHEET

When it comes to baking pizza at home, an aluminum sheet pan is merely serviceable. Your pizza will lack the crisp crust of pizza baked on steel, but it will taste good, and you'll still get points for making the dough!

BAKING STONE

This heavy, flat stone absorbs heat from your oven and allows you to bake pizza right on top of it. This ensures that your pizza is cooked evenly, but good luck getting the crunchy bite and flavorful charred bottom of your favorite brick-oven pies.

BAKING STEEL

Like a baking stone, the Baking Steel absorbs heat from the oven. But the Baking Steel's alloy has a thermal conductivity eighteen times greater than a ceramic pizza stone's, so your pizza bakes faster and at higher heat. This gives you a professional-looking pie with a crisper crust, a satisfying crunch, and perfect hints of char.

knees, not your back. There are many different Baking Steel models, but they're all heavy!

HEATING AND COOLING YOUR STEEL

Part of the magic of the Baking Steel is that the even heat distribution ensures even cooking and baking. To help the steel do its best work, you'll need to allow it to heat up properly. The steel is equally effective for cold tasks, like mixing cold slab ice cream or serving sushi. Follow these instructions to preheat or precool the steel.

Pizza: Place the Baking Steel in the top rack of your oven (or about six inches from the broiler). Set the oven to its highest temperature; this is often 500 degrees, though some ovens can go higher. If your oven has a convection setting, use it, though it's not vital for success. Let your Baking Steel preheat in the oven for forty-five minutes to an hour to allow it to absorb the heat. Always use a pizza peel to launch your pie onto the steel and to remove it; never touch the hot steel directly. For more detailed information on the process of baking pizza with your Baking Steel, see page 19.

Bread and Other Baked Goods: Place the Baking Steel in the oven; you will usually put it on the middle rack unless otherwise noted. Let it preheat for forty-five minutes to an hour at the temperature called for in the recipe—this allows the steel to completely absorb the heat required for those perfectly crispy edges. As always, do not touch the Baking Steel at any time; put your baked goods on a sheet of parchment paper and use a pizza peel to launch them onto the steel, or place a baking sheet on top of the steel and take care to avoid contact with the steel when removing it, as it can burn you even through oven mitts.

Roasting / Cooking: Preheat your Baking Steel as recommended for bread and baking, above. Often, these recipes employ a rimmed sheet tray positioned on top of the steel to prevent drips.

Griddle-Top Cooking: Several of the recipes in this book are cooked using the Baking Steel Griddle directly on top of your stove. Here's how to successfully heat your Baking Steel Griddle on the stovetop for even cooking.

1. *Mise en place.* Make sure that you have all of your cooking materials close at hand and remove anything near the stovetop that may be sensitive to heat.

2. *Place the steel directly on top of your stove burners.* Position it carefully, as you won't want to move or touch it directly once it gets hot.

3. *Turn on the heat.* Start high; I like to start heating on medium-high, even if I need a fairly low temperature for whatever I'm making. Let your Baking Steel heat for ten to fifteen minutes. An instant-read infrared thermometer (easily obtained at better

cookware stores and online) is handy for determining the heat of the surface before you cook. Without one, you might find it difficult to monitor and maintain a steady temperature. As you'll see, each griddle recipe has a suggested temperature range. As you become more adept at cooking on the surface, you will learn how long it takes to reach the appropriate level of heat, and you can adjust accordingly in the recipes.

4. *Lower the heat.* Right before you put whatever you're cooking on the surface, lower the heat to medium. In general, this will keep the temperature from continuing to rise and will allow you to maintain the suggested cooking temperature. Keep track of the temperature using that infrared thermometer.

5. *Get cooking!* Place your food on the steel and let it do its magic.

6. *Let the Baking Steel cool down.* Once you're done, turn off the heat and let the steel sit on the stovetop until cool enough to handle. Don't attempt to move it right after cooking, as you could burn yourself.

Ice Cream: Put the steel in the freezer and leave it there overnight (as you would an ice cream maker drum).

Sushi and Other Chilled Foods: To keep your cold foods cold at a party or cookout, put the steel in the freezer for at least twenty minutes and up to several hours before you use it.

HANDLING YOUR STEEL

Your Baking Steel might not look hot in the oven, but trust me—it is very, *very* hot. Once you've heated your Baking Steel in your oven or on your stovetop, you should *never* touch it; it can burn you even through oven mitts.

If you've chilled your Baking Steel in the refrigerator or freezer, wear oven mitts when removing it.

After baking or cooking on it, allow it ample time to cool down before handling. While exact times will vary, it can take up to an hour to become cool enough to handle.

CLEANING YOUR BAKING STEEL

As your Baking Steel ages, you'll notice some changes. The color will darken with each use, and the steel will eventually develop a very dark or black patina. Just as with cast-iron cookware, this isn't a bad thing, nor is it a sign that your Baking Steel is on its last legs. As long as you keep your Baking Steel clean and re-season it occasionally, it will last a lifetime.

EVERYDAY CARE

After using the Baking Steel or Baking Steel Griddle, let it cool completely before handling it. Once it's cool, employ a bench scraper to scrape food matter into the sink. Once you've cleared off any food debris, wash your Baking Steel with soap and water. Although using soap on cast-iron cookware is a no-no, using soap on your Baking Steel—and even scrubbing, as long as it's with nothing harsher than the back of a sponge—is perfectly okay. Be sure to dry both sides thoroughly and immediately every time your Baking Steel gets wet; never let it air-dry, as this can promote rust. And never put your Baking Steel in the dishwasher.

Oil the Baking Steel with a neutral, food-grade oil after every cleaning; this keeps the surface nonstick and creates a seal that keeps rust from forming. If you are used to caring for a cast-iron pan, taking care of your Baking Steel is no different in this regard.

DEEPER CLEANING

If you've left your Baking Steel in the oven for a while or if you forgot to dry it immediately, rust spots may form. A deeper cleaning will be needed, but there's no need to panic. Run to your local grocery store and pick up a product called Bar Keepers Friend. Place a small amount of this product on a slightly wet Baking Steel, let it sit for about one minute, and then rinse the steel clean. Use a little soap and water to clean it once again, and then carefully dry your Baking Steel. Always re-season your steel after using Bar Keepers Friend; the process is detailed below.

Another product for cleaning stubborn rust spots or stains is the Earthstone KitchenStone brick. Made from 95 percent recycled glass, these cleaning bricks are all natural and nontoxic and have the cleaning power of something like forty Brillo pads. They're well worth the investment for removing tough, stuck-on food from your Baking Steel or Baking Steel Griddle.

To clean with the scrubbing brick, simply scour the dry Baking Steel until clean. Try to avoid using water; if it is needed, use a very small amount. Wipe the surface lightly to remove loose residue.

If for some reason your Baking Steel develops a metallic smell or taste or you notice rust spots (maybe well-meaning relatives washed your Baking Steel in the dishwasher, thinking they were being helpful), don't panic. Simply scour off the rust using steel wool or very fine sandpaper and re-season as below.

RE-SEASONING YOUR BAKING STEEL

While the Baking Steel arrives seasoned, it will require occasional re-seasoning. In general, if you notice that its surface is looking dull and gray or that food is constantly sticking to it, it's time to re-season.

1. Position a rack in the middle of your oven. Preheat the oven to 400°F.

2. Wash the Baking Steel with hot, soapy water and a stiff brush.

3. Rinse and dry immediately and completely.

4. Apply a dab of neutral oil (I suggest Barlean's organic flaxseed oil) in the center of the Baking Steel. Using a paper towel, wipe the oil around the steel evenly. Use another paper towel and wipe off excess. Do this to both sides. It will appear to have a thin, light sheen from the oil.

5. Place the Baking Steel in the preheated oven.

6. Keep the Baking Steel in the oven for 1 hour. When the hour is up, turn off the oven and leave the steel there until it's cool enough to move.

OTHER HANDY INFO

Parchment paper: If you're worried about drips, parchment paper is a great alternative to launching food directly onto the Baking Steel, and it allows for quick and easy removal of whatever you are baking. Typically, I use parchment paper when I make stromboli, slab pies, and calzones. Now, most parchment-paper packaging will say that it's suggested for use only up to 400 degrees. Well, I've used it many times with a much hotter Baking Steel, and while it turns brown and wrinkles, it has never caught fire. Do *not*, however, use parchment paper under the broiler.

Silicone mats: It's okay to use a silicone mat on top of the Baking Steel, but only to the maximum temperature suggested by the mat's manufacturer. As with parchment, do not use silicone mats under the broiler.

Baking pans: You can put baking sheets, cake pans, and pie plates right on top of your Baking Steel. Even though whatever you're making is separated from the direct surface of the steel, the steel will still conduct heat evenly through the sheet or pan to give it a perfectly crisped bottom.

Removing grease from your Baking Steel Griddle: When you cook bacon or meat on top of your Baking Steel Griddle, grease or juices can get caught in the channel around the perimeter. To remove, let the griddle cool somewhat so that you don't burn yourself. Dab paper towels around the channel to remove anything that might slosh, then wait until the Baking Steel Griddle cools down completely to clean more thoroughly. Be careful—that steel gets very hot!

Storing your Baking Steel: We sell every Baking Steel with a storage sleeve, and that's probably the best place to keep it once it's completely dry and coated in a thin layer of oil. However, many people simply leave the Baking Steel in the oven and cook everything on top of it. If you do this, you may notice that it becomes very dark, but that's okay. Just be sure to remove it from time to time so you can clean and re-season it.

Baking Steel or Baking Steel Griddle? There are two key differences between the Baking Steel and the Baking Steel Griddle. One is texture; the Baking Steel surface is lightly textured, whereas the Baking Steel Griddle is smooth. The griddle also features a channel around the perimeter to capture grease or excess liquid. You can use both cooking surfaces interchangeably in many recipes. However, it is suggested that you don't use the Baking Steel on your stovetop for recipes that could get messy or that might result in grease dripping off.

2
PIZZA

2

MAKING PIZZA
THE BAKING STEEL WAY

Welcome to the pizza-making adventure of a lifetime. Here is your road map to the basic technique for baking a pizza on steel, as well as a breakdown of the tools and ingredients that will help make every pie perfection.

PIZZA ON STEEL: THE BASIC TECHNIQUE

Preheating your Baking Steel for making pizza requires a specific process and a little time. Don't worry; you'll get used to it fast. Be sure to follow these instructions to ensure that your Baking Steel is properly heated and primed to help you make the perfect pizza.

1. **Assume the position.** Place the Baking Steel on the top rack of your oven, or about six inches below the broiler, unless the recipe specifies otherwise.

2. **Set the temperature.** Unless the recipe specifies a particular temperature, set the oven to the highest possible temperature (often 500 degrees—if your oven goes higher, go for it!) and let the Baking Steel preheat for forty-five minutes to an hour; it must fully heat to ensure that you get a crispy crust. If you have a convection setting on your oven, employ it; if you don't, it's not necessary.

3. **Set the oven to Broil.** In most of the pizza recipes, I call for setting the oven on Broil shortly before launching the pie onto the Baking Steel. This initial blast of heat helps the crust set on the bottom and makes the toppings start to crisp.

4. **Get baking!** With your oven on Broil, launch your pizza onto the hot Baking Steel using a pizza peel. (You should absolutely not handle the steel once it's hot.) Let the pizza cook for two minutes under the broiler, then turn off the broiler and set the oven to its highest temperature.

5. **Remove with care.** Once the pizza is cooked to your liking, remove it from the oven using a pizza peel.

6. **Let it cool.** Let the steel cool completely in the oven before handling. This can take up to a few hours.

Peel to Steel: Removing the Fear of the Transfer

A pizza peel is essentially a flat shovel that you use to transfer a pizza to and from the cooking surface. This process can be daunting to newbies; here are some tips to keep you from experiencing "failure to launch."

MAKE SURE IT'S BIG ENOUGH. It's common sense: Your peel has to be large enough to fit your entire pizza. I like to assemble my pizza on top of the peel so that I can make sure it's the correct size. My favorite peel measures fourteen inches in diameter, and its handle is approximately four inches.

MATERIAL MATTERS. I like a wooden pizza peel because the pizza tends to slide off it a bit easier than it does with a metal variety.

JUST DO IT. Like when you invert a cake or flip pancakes, take a deep breath and just do it! If you launch too slowly, your toppings can slosh over the edge.

HAVE SOME FRIENDS NEARBY. For one thing, they provide moral support. For another, if you find your pizza stuck, they can help get the pizza off the peel with spatulas.

IF THINGS DO GO WRONG... Let's say half your toppings slither onto the steel when you launch your pizza. Just let it cook and then later remove it the best you can; it's easier to remove toppings after the steel cools than it is to do it while the steel is hot. The occasional kitchen catastrophe is inevitable, but you don't have to let it ruin your day. Just keep the local pizzeria's number close at hand; at least you'll have something to talk about while you wait for your order.

FROM PEEL TO STEEL

There are a few ways to lubricate the bottom of the pizza for easier transfer to the oven. Dust your peel before stretching your dough and assembling your pizza on it.

- Semolina is a fantastic lubricant and adds a slightly nutty flavor to your pizza.
- Cornmeal adds fascinating flavor, but it burns more rapidly than flour or semolina, so use sparingly.
- Flour is what I favor because I always have it on hand from making the dough.

TOOLS

Now that you've got the technique down, you're going to need a little help from your friends, and by that, I mean the proper pizza-making tools and gadgets.

DIGITAL KITCHEN SCALES

I cannot overemphasize the importance of using a kitchen scale in your baking. Measuring your dry ingredients by weight is the only way to attain the proper ratios. In baking—and particularly to achieve a sensational pizza crust—these are crucial.

When you measure flour with a measuring cup and not by weight, the amount of flour can differ from day to day depending on a host of factors, including the weather. While leveling off cups of flour can get you a decent result, it's not a precise art. And if you want perfection, you need to get your ingredient ratios right every time. That said, for dry ingredients, we've included both volume and weight measurements in these recipes; liquid measurements are given by volume.

A **basic digital kitchen scale** will be sensitive enough for dry ingredients used in large amounts, like flour, but you'll also need to measure ingredients used in smaller amounts, like tenths of a gram of yeast, and most digital scales aren't precise enough to measure fractions of a gram. For that, you'll need a **microscale** (also called a jeweler's scale). You can pick one up on Amazon for twenty dollars or less. There are even devices that have both macro- and microscale capabilities.

Be sure to employ the Tare setting on your scale. Once you set your bowl on the scale surface, hit Tare (sometimes marked Zero) to bring the scale back to zero. This lets you weigh the contents of the bowl and not the bowl itself!

PEELS

If you're using a wooden peel, always keep it dry, the way you would a butcher block. Rub mineral oil on it and treat it well, and it will last forever.

Don't get a peel that is larger than your Baking Steel; it will be cumbersome to transfer the pizza onto the steel.

Oh, and another bonus to having a good pizza peel: you can use your peel as your serving platter—remove the pizza from the oven, then slice it right there. How easy is that?

CUTTERS

I suggest a pizza rocker—a large, curved blade with handles on both sides. It looks sort of like a torture device, but it's super-handy when cutting pizza; it's faster than a roller, and you can get a more consistent (and Instagram-worthy) cut.

If you're a traditionalist, standard pizza rollers are cheap and readily available at kitchen-supply stores. Choose one that is sturdy and that you can handle confidently.

STORAGE CONTAINERS AND OTHER TOOLS

If you want to make round pizzas, store your dough in round containers. Keep round Tupperware or Pyrex flat-bottomed bowls with fitted lids on hand. You'll also need a cutting board, a sturdy wire whisk for mixing, and a blender or food processor.

OPTIONAL: ROLLING PIN

When I worked at Figs, we shaped our dough with a rolling pin. For a long time, I continued this practice, and I even used it in our Kickstarter promo video. Viewers gave me a hard time about this; basically, their comments boiled down to *Genuine pizzaiolos do not use rolling pins to shape their dough. They stretch it by hand.*

These days, I rarely use a rolling pin unless I need to knock air bubbles out of the dough. But you should begin with what works for you. If you find it easier to use a rolling pin, proceed without shame! (See more dough-stretching instructions on page 30.)

INGREDIENTS

Even if you have the right tools and the proper technique, your pizza will never be great without the right ingredients.

HIGH-PROTEIN FLOUR

The key to perfect pizza dough is high-protein flour, which is why many of our doughs call for bread flour. The higher the protein, the sturdier the dough, meaning it can stand up to the kneading and stretching necessary to create a great crust.

My go-to flour is Central Milling High Mountain flour, which is available online. It's pricey, but worth every penny. If you want a brand you can find in just about any grocery store, I suggest King Arthur bread flour. It has a protein content of 12.7 percent, higher than what you'll find in most all-purpose flours (which hover around 9 percent) as well as in many other brands of bread flour. The percentage of protein doesn't vary much; King Arthur allows for only a 0.2 percent variance in protein content, while other commercial flour makers allow for a 2.0 percent variance or even higher. It may not seem like much, but that decimal point makes a big difference! Higher amounts of protein can lead to denser, chewier dough, but too much makes your dough overly dry and tough.

VITAL WHEAT GLUTEN

If you don't want to stock multiple types of flour in your pantry, pick up some vital wheat gluten. (Bob's Red Mill is a dependable brand.) It basically transforms all-purpose flour into bread flour by adding protein to it—about one tablespoon per five hundred grams of flour. Don't try to amp up your bread flour, though, because too much protein will make your crust tough to chew.

SALT

You may not find salt in every recipe for pizza dough. But have you ever tasted a crust made without salt? A properly salted dough enhances each ingredient in a pizza. Unless otherwise noted, I suggest fine sea salt for my recipes. Its texture distributes better than more coarse salts, although regular sea salt is fine in a pinch.

TOMATOES

I like canned tomatoes better than fresh on my pizza because they retain more of the pure essence of tomato flavor. Fresh tomatoes can be too wet and bland in a pizza, so

I like to get the best of both worlds by adding fresh tomatoes to my sauce! My favorite canned variety is Bianco DiNapoli's whole peeled tomatoes. I simply break them up by hand and call it sauce.

Cheese Tips

- Use cold cheese. If the cheese is already warm, it can brown too quickly and throw off the doneness of the pie.

- Avoid liquid or processed cheeses (sorry, Velveeta!). They drip and make an oily mess.

- Add hard cheeses, like Parmesan, after the pizza comes out of the oven. Think of them as finishing spices. When shredded, they will melt quickly on top of a hot pizza.

- Avoid pre-grated cheese, which is often packed with starch to prevent it from clumping. That starch can brown more rapidly than the cheese and give a false indication of doneness.

- Use whole-milk cheese whenever possible; the milk fat imparts more flavor and keeps the cheese from browning too quickly.

LOW-MOISTURE WHOLE-MILK MOZZARELLA

The most common cheese on pizza. It's a classic for a reason. Just make sure you buy blocks of it, not the pre-shredded stuff in bags.

FRESH MOZZARELLA

Be sure to dry the cheese completely before topping a pie with it. Either blot it thoroughly with paper towels or use cheesecloth to press the excess liquid out. When mozzarella is wet, it can form a weirdly gummy texture with the sauce. It will taste fine, but it's probably not the visual you're going for. Tear the mozzarella ball into pieces by hand and space them in fairly regular intervals across the crust. I like to buy local fresh mozzarella whenever possible; here in New England, Vermont's Maplebrook Farm is a personal favorite.

OTHER MELTING CHEESES

Cheddar, provolone, Gouda, Asiago, Colby, fontina, Gruyère, Havarti, Monterey Jack, and Muenster can also be allies in your pizza journey. Don't be afraid to try different combinations! All of these will melt well and crisp up nicely.

CREAMY CHEESES

Creamy cheeses like ricotta, cream cheese, and fresh goat cheese can be a nice alternative to the usual. Drop dollops evenly across the stretched dough. Keep them cold before you use them so they don't spread too much in the oven and drip.

AGED HARD CHEESES

Parmesan (Parmigiano-Reggiano) and Pecorino Romano are delicious, but they don't melt like other cheeses, so use them to add flavor to an already-baked pie.

OLIVE OIL

Keep a good extra-virgin olive oil on hand for your pizza making. It can be used to oil your hands for kneading or handling sticky dough if necessary, and it's wonderful as a finishing flavor. I like to keep mine in a squirt bottle, restaurant-style, to give a quick finishing drizzle around the perimeter of the pizza as it comes out of the oven. The aroma and flavor will hit you on the first bite. This is a moment to use the good stuff.

DOUGH: THE FOUNDATION OF GREAT PIZZA

Pizza is made up of three key components: dough, sauce, and cheese. Simple, right? Well, yes and no. If you're a pizza nerd (and if you've found this book, you probably are), dough gets more interesting the more you explore it.

I dabble with fermentation times, add liquids other than water, mess with the amount of yeast, and always find it fun (and delicious) to taste the sometimes subtle, sometimes major flavor differences. In this chapter, I'll show you how to create a variety of great basic doughs and give you the opportunity to experiment with them.

If you really want to geek out with dough, be sure that you have a digital scale and a microscale (see Tools). It's what the pros do, and not just because owning two scales sounds cool. It helps you attain the exacting ratios that make crusts work, and that's how you'll be able to replicate the finest restaurant pizzas at home.

THE BAKER'S PERCENTAGE: A DOUGH MASTER'S SECRET WEAPON

I have a deep distrust of dough recipes that don't call for weight measurements. This is not out of pizza snobbery; it's to prevent lousy, inconsistent results. If you and I each measured four cups of flour, your four cups would actually contain a different amount of flour than my four cups. This depends on a multitude of small but significant factors: the temperature and humidity outside, how long your flour has been sitting, how firmly you pack it in the cup, and so on. Flour does not have a constant density, so measuring it by volume (with a measuring cup) is much less accurate than measuring it by weight (with a scale). But I'm not trying to tell you how to live your life, so all of the recipes in this book include both weight and volume measurements so that you can follow the method that feels natural to you.

Making dough is ultimately a science, and all doughs rely on what is called the baker's percentage. This means the flour's relative proportion to other ingredients in bread, cakes, pastries, pie crust, and, yes, pizza dough. Every ingredient is based on its relationship to the flour weight. Take a look at this typical pizza-dough recipe.

500 grams of flour	100 percent (because every other ingredient is in relation to the flour)
350 grams of water	70 percent (because 350 divided by 500 is 0.7, or 70 percent)
16 grams fine sea salt	3.2 percent
1 gram yeast	.002 percent

Memorize these percentages and you can scale a batch of dough up or down whenever you like. Take note of the amount of total liquid; this is called the hydration level. And while it seems infinitesimal, it's important to pay close attention to the yeast portion, that .002 percent. Aren't you glad you bought that microscale now?

As you get comfortable making dough, start experimenting. Play around with the percentages. Our basic dough recipe has a hydration level of 70 percent, making the dough very sticky and somewhat difficult to handle. Change the hydration level (amount of water) to 60 percent and you may find that stretching the dough is a bit easier, but it will have slightly less spring, bubbles, and buoyancy.

Once you're familiar with baker's percentages, you'll be able to dissect and compare recipes. Pizza dough is always a high-hydration dough—usually between 60 and 70 percent—and we like to keep our yeast no higher than 1 percent, and usually much lower. Any more is just not necessary.

If this all seems intimidating, don't worry. These are the tools you'll need to become a pizza rock star at home, but you don't have to improvise right away.

DOUGH BASICS

Before you start mixing your first batch of dough, there are some things you knead—er, need—to know. With this information and a few basic techniques under your belt, you'll be prepared to make the perfect crust.

Which Dough Should I Make?

First you need to decide what type of pizza crust you want and when you want to eat your pizza. Because the yeast in pizza dough needs time to ferment (fermenting creates those bubbles in the crust we so admire and causes more complex flavor to develop), time is very important to the process. You can have great pizza tonight, but if you think ahead, you can have unimaginably good pizza three days from now.

As far as the crust goes, in this book you can generally mix and match your favorite recipe with whatever toppings you'd like. While I default to the foundational Seventy-Two-Hour Pizza Dough on many recipes, you can feel free to choose your own adventure; only in certain cases, such as the stromboli or the calzone, will I make specific suggestions. The key differences will lie in how much dough you use and how far you stretch it out. For instance, the Seventy-Two-Hour Pizza Dough ball can be divided into four smaller balls so you can make four small thin-crust pies, but you'll need the whole dough ball to make a sheet tray of the more robustly crusted Spicy Sicilian Pizza.

Making Dough Balls

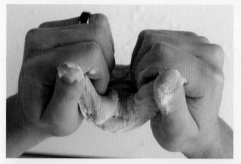

1. Place one dough portion between your hands and fold in the edges by pressing them into the center of the dough. This is going to be the seam side. The opposite side should look smooth and seamless.

2. With the seam side facing away from you, rotate the ball ninety degrees. Gather and fold the edges into the center of the dough ball again.

3. Repeat this process about fifteen times (that sounds like a lot, but as you get used to it, you'll work fast).

4. Place the smooth side in your palm and swiftly pinch the seam closed. Be aggressive with the pinch.

5. Place each dough ball into an oiled, cylindrical airtight container (deli-takeaway containers are ideal), date it, and put in the fridge for forty-eight to ninety-six hours.

6. Remove from the refrigerator at least one hour before use to allow the dough to come to room temperature; this lets the gluten relax and makes the dough malleable.

Shaping and Stretching Dough

Once your dough is properly shaped into balls, you want to stretch it into the perfect pizza canvas.

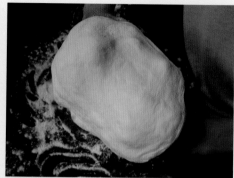

1. Remove the dough from the refrigerator about one hour before shaping. Let it rest and come to room temperature so that it is malleable. Err on the side of letting your dough sit at room temperature for slightly too long rather than not long enough, as room-temperature dough is easier to stretch than cold dough.

2. Remove any rings with stones or edges that might catch the dough (a wedding band with no stones is fine, though). Generously flour your work surface and your hands. Turn your dough container upside down and, using your fingertips, gently coax it out. The oil in the container will help. Place the dough, oil-side down, in the flour and gently turn it over so that both sides are generously floured.

3. Place the dough ball on your work surface and press down. Work your fingers outward as you press so that the dough expands and flattens but remains circular. Be gentle; you don't want to knock out all of those precious bubbles, which give your crust buoyancy. Keep working the dough outward until it's about six inches in diameter.

4. Lift the dough off your work surface, form your hands into loose fists, and place the dough on top of your knuckles. Once the dough is in position, rotate and stretch it on the back of your knuckles in one direction. Continue to pull it wider and wider with each rotation, but don't pull too hard; you're mainly letting gravity do its thing. Keep going until you've reached your desired diameter.

5. Now you're ready to place the dough on your floured or lubricated peel and assemble your pizza.

Blister, Don't Burn: How to Attain the Perfect Blistered Crust

The Baking Steel will help you produce the perfect pizza crust all by itself, but with time and experimentation, we've figured out some tricks. If you want to get a perfectly blistered crust that is 100 percent Instagram-worthy, try these methods.

If You Have a Gas Oven: Gas ovens are my preferred oven for pizza making. They're quick to jump to attention; as soon as you turn on the broiler, it's ready to go. But use caution—if you leave that broiler on for too long, your Baking Steel will hit temperatures upwards of 700 degrees Fahrenheit, which is too hot for pizza dough in a home oven. That's why we suggest that you don't turn on the broiler until just before you launch, and that's why it's left on for only the first two minutes of baking.

If You Have an Electric Oven: An electric oven is definitely "smarter," or more regulated, than a gas oven. If you turn on the broiler in an electric oven, it'll be a few minutes before it's ready. It might take a while for you to figure out exactly when you need to turn on the broiler before you launch, as the speed of the broiler heating can vary.

If You Have a Bottom-Drawer Broiler: This style of oven is rare these days, but you'll still see it in some older homes. If you have this type of broiler, we have a hack for making your pizza perfect. You'll preheat your Baking Steel as suggested in the recipe. Launch your pizza and cook for four to five minutes. Remove the pizza, switch the oven to Broil, and place it in the bottom drawer, under the broiler, for thirty to forty-five seconds. That will give you some nice color on top of your pizza.

Advanced: Use Two Steels

This method comes from a highly reputable source: Tony Gemignani, a twelve-time World Pizza Cup champion. Start by placing two Baking Steels in your oven, one on a higher rack, one on a lower rack, with enough space to launch a pizza onto both.

Preheat your oven. Then, before you stretch out your dough (or about five minutes before launching your pizza onto the steel), switch the oven setting to Broil (High Broil, if that's an option). Launch the pizza onto the top rack and let it cook for two minutes. Then transfer the pizza to the lower rack and change the oven back to regular or convection setting at the highest temperature. Your results will be out of this world.

A Note on Bubbles: Should you pop them? Bubbles will typically rise and get larger under some heat, so they will tend to burn in the oven. I think that adds character to a pizza and makes it unique, so I let 'em stay. If you prefer a more seamless pie, go ahead and pop them when rotating your pizza during baking.

SEVENTY-TWO-HOUR PIZZA DOUGH

One of my favorite pizza-dough recipes is Jim Lahey's no-knead dough, on which this recipe is based. It's simple, doesn't require any equipment, and doesn't make a big mess. (My wife disagrees about the mess; I have a talent for covering the kitchen in flour.) I make this dough at least once a week, sometimes quintupling the recipe and saving the extra balls of dough to use later or for the pizza classes I teach.

Through the years, I have adapted Jim's original recipe to make it my own. One change is that I use bread flour instead of all-purpose flour, which adds the perfect heft to your crust when the dough is baked at high heat in a home environment. And somewhat ironically, I actually knead the no-knead dough. After I incorporate all the ingredients, I wet my hands and knead the batch for two to three minutes. Without this step, I've ended up with dried clumps of flour in the dough. There are worse things in life, but we're seekers of pizza perfection.

This dough is simple and foolproof, but you do need *time*. Not hands-on or working time, but twenty-four hours for rising and then forty-eight hours for the cold ferment. That's seventy-two hours total, in case you don't have a calculator.

The first twenty-four hours allows the dough to bulk ferment (or rise as one unit before being divided into individual dough portions) at room temperature; just park the dough someplace where it won't be disturbed. The dough will release a pleasant aroma that will make your kitchen smell like a bakery.

Next, you'll portion out the dough, ball it up, and store the balls in the refrigerator for a minimum of one day and up to ten. This is when the dough will develop some kick-ass flavor. The process is called cold fermentation, and it slows down the activity of the yeast to produce amazing flavors in your dough. The strike zone for the dough, in terms of optimal texture and flavor, is from day three through day five (or forty-eight to ninety-six hours after the bulk fermentation that occurs in step 4). You can take the dough out of the fridge and make pizza earlier, but the full seventy-two-hour method is what gives it a truly memorable taste and texture.

MAKES FOUR 10-INCH PIES, THREE 12- TO 14-INCH PIES, OR ONE 18-BY-13-INCH SICILIAN PIE

500 grams (3¾ cups) bread flour

16 grams (1 tablespoon) fine sea salt

1 gram (¼ teaspoon) active dry yeast

1½ cups water, at room temperature

1. In a large bowl, whisk together the bread flour, salt, and yeast.

2. Slowly add the water and mix with a wooden spoon just to combine. Once the mixture is moistened, lightly flour a countertop or large cutting board and remove the dough from the bowl with lightly oiled or wet hands (to discourage sticking).

Knead for 2 to 3 minutes to remove clumps. The dough won't become elastic but should easily form a loose ball.

3. Place the dough in a lightly oiled bowl and cover with a damp, clean kitchen towel or plastic wrap to prevent it from drying out.

4. Place the bowl on the counter and let sit 24 hours at room temperature. It will double in size and you may see bubbles forming on the surface.

5. Lightly flour a large cutting board or your kitchen countertop and place the dough on it. Wet or lightly oil your hands again.

6. Divide dough into 4 equal portions for 10-inch pies or 3 portions if you're making slightly larger pies. If making Spicy Sicilian Pizza (page 82), do not divide the dough. With wet or oiled hands, make each portion into a dough ball (see page 29).

7. Place the dough balls into oiled, cylindrical airtight containers (deli-takeaway containers are ideal), date them, and place in the fridge for 48 to 96 hours.

8. Remove from refrigerator at least 1 hour before use to allow the dough to come to room temperature; this lets the gluten relax and makes the dough malleable.

ONE MASTER DOUGH, INFINITE VARIATIONS

Peak period of fermentation: The peak period for making pizza with this dough is between forty-eight and ninety-six hours after the initial bulk ferment, when the dough doubles in size. (If you start the dough on Tuesday, prime pizza time will be Friday through Sunday.) Feel free to experiment with fermentation times until you find what works best for you.

Alternative liquids: You can substitute other liquids for the water called for in this recipe in a one-to-one ratio. Beer adds a nice, malty touch; a little milk will make your dough extra-rich. If you're feeling crazy, try something like coffee—really! Coffee in a dessert-pizza crust elevates you to a culinary genius.

Alternative flours: Try the Whole-Wheat Pizza Dough on page 36 and experiment by swapping other flours, like oat flour or rye, for a small amount (a half a cup or so) of the bread flour.

Freezing: You can freeze this dough until you are ready to use it or if you have leftovers. Let the dough ferment to its peak period (as mentioned above, forty-eight to ninety-six hours in the fridge), then place in an airtight container to freeze for up to two months. Put it in the refrigerator to thaw the night before you plan on using it, then let it come to room temperature for an hour before stretching it. If you forget to remove the dough the night before, don't panic. Remove it from the freezer and place it on the counter for a few hours before making the pizza.

WHOLE-WHEAT PIZZA DOUGH

Whole-Wheat Pizza Dough is a win-win situation. The addition of whole wheat adds nutty, complex flavor while increasing the overall healthiness of your pie. It has been one of our most requested recipes, and after much trial and error, we've found the perfect combination of ingredients. I adjusted our Seventy-Two-Hour Pizza Dough (page 32) by substituting whole-wheat flour for part (not all) of the bread flour. This dough is a little less springy because of the higher density of the whole-wheat flour, but it delivers a crispy, flavorful, healthier pizza crust.

MAKES FOUR 10-INCH PIES
OR THREE 12- TO 14-INCH PIES

400 grams (3¼ cups) bread flour

100 grams (about ¾ cup) whole-wheat flour

1 gram (¼ teaspoon) active dry yeast

16 grams (1 tablespoon) fine sea salt

1½ cups water, at room temperature

1. In a large bowl, whisk together the bread flour, whole-wheat flour, yeast, and salt.

2. Slowly add the water and mix with a wooden spoon just to combine. Once the mixture is moistened, lightly flour a countertop or large cutting board and remove the dough from the bowl with lightly oiled or wet hands. Knead for 2 to 3 minutes to remove clumps. The dough won't become elastic but should easily form a loose ball.

3. Place the dough in a lightly oiled bowl and cover with a damp, clean kitchen towel or plastic wrap.

4. Let the dough sit at room temperature for 24 hours. It will double in size, and you may see air bubbles forming on the surface.

5. Lightly flour a large cutting board or your kitchen countertop and place the dough on it. Wet or lightly oil your hands again.

6. Divide the dough into 4 equal portions for 10-inch pies or 3 portions if you're making slightly larger pies. With wet or oiled hands, roll each portion into a dough ball (page 29).

7. Place the dough balls into lightly oiled, cylindrical airtight containers (deli-takeaway containers are ideal), date them, and place in the fridge for up to 5 days.

8. Remove the dough from the refrigerator at least 1 hour before using to allow the dough to come to room temperature; this lets the gluten relax and makes the dough malleable.

SOURDOUGH PIZZA DOUGH

Sourdough isn't just for sandwiches and oversize bread bowls. A sourdough crust instantly makes your pizza gourmet. Sourdough is made by the long fermentation of dough using naturally occurring lactobacilli and yeasts. This long fermentation gives the sourdough starter a pleasingly funky taste, and it adds a tangy, irresistible flavor to pizza dough.

While Sourdough Pizza Dough is relatively easy to make, it requires a time commitment. Because of the specific feeding process required to cultivate your sourdough starter, it's going to be about a week from start to pizza. The beginning of this recipe is similar to our classic Seventy-Two-Hour Pizza Dough, but instead of adding dry yeast, we add 20 percent of the dough's weight in a natural starter, or *biga* (a firm mixture of water, flour, and yeast). The result is a naturally leavened crust with that inimitable sourdough tang.

**MAKES FOUR 10-INCH PIES
OR THREE 12- TO 14-INCH PIES**

500 grams (3¾ cups) bread flour	1 cup water
16 grams (1 tablespoon) fine sea salt	½ cup sourdough starter (recipe follows)

1. In a large bowl, whisk the flour and salt together.

2. Slowly add the water and mix with a wooden spoon just to combine.

3. With lightly oiled or wet hands, remove the dough from the bowl, place on a lightly floured surface, and knead in the sourdough starter for 2 to 3 minutes to remove any clumps. The dough won't become elastic but should easily form a loose ball.

4. Place the dough in a lightly oiled bowl and cover with a damp, clean kitchen towel or plastic wrap to prevent it from drying out.

5. Place on counter and let sit 24 hours at room temperature. It will double in size and you may see bubbles forming on the surface.

6. Lightly flour a large cutting board or countertop and turn the dough out on it. Wet or lightly oil your hands again.

7. Divide dough into 4 equal portions (or 3 if you're making slightly larger pies) and form each portion into a dough ball.

8. Place each dough ball in a lightly oiled, cylindrical airtight container and label with the date. Refrigerate for up to 5 days.

9. Remove the dough from the refrigerator 1 hour before using it to allow the dough to come to room temperature.

SOURDOUGH STARTER

Naturally leavened doughs are made without the addition of commercial yeast (that is, the kind you buy at the grocery store). Instead, they are given their lift from the growth of naturally occurring yeasts around us. Some of the best bakeries and pizzerias in the country use natural leaveners or sourdough starters to create their doughs.

Making and maintaining a sourdough starter is like taking care of a hardy houseplant—it requires only occasional upkeep. Every few weeks, you discard part of the starter mixture and feed the rest with fresh flour and water.

To get your culture (starter) going, you are going to need a few things: time (about five days), a mason jar with a lid, whole-wheat flour, and water. We like to start with whole-wheat flour because it has more nutrients than typical white or bread flour. Once you get the starter going, you can substitute bread flour.

To start

⅔ cup water, at room temperature

150 grams (slightly more than 1 cup) whole-wheat flour

To feed

130 grams (1 cup) whole-wheat flour

½ cup water, at room temperature

1. In a medium-size bowl, mix the water and the whole-wheat flour thoroughly with a wooden spoon. Place in an airtight container (I use a mason jar, though any airtight container will work) and keep at room temperature for 24 hours. It may begin to bubble slightly. I like to keep it in my (turned-off) oven, because when the door is sealed, it creates even more of a vacuum than the airtight container alone, and a relatively warm, temperature-controlled space is perfect for developing the starter. You could also keep it in a microwave. Just make sure that you don't accidentally turn on the oven or microwave before removing your starter!

2. After 24 hours, discard half of the starter mixture and add 130 grams of flour and ½ cup of water; this is known as feeding your starter. Mix with a wooden spoon and let sit for another 24 hours in the same environment. Repeat the process daily for 5 days. The mixture will become more active and bubbly as you go.

3. After 5 days, your starter is active and ready. If you're not going to use it right away, put the starter in your refrigerator and continue to feed on a weekly basis by discarding half the mixture and adding 130 grams of flour and ½ cup of water.

4. To use, remove from fridge, discard half, and feed one last time, then leave at room temperature until it becomes active and bubbly, about 24 hours.

GLUTEN-FREE PIZZA DOUGH

If you love pizza but your body doesn't love gluten, it need not be an insurmountable problem. This Gluten-Free Pizza Dough proves that you can have pizza and stay gluten-free too.

There are a few different approaches to making a gluten-free crust. One is simply to use a gluten-free flour mix, such as Cup4Cup, substituting it in equal quantities for all-purpose flour. You can make that substitution in any of the recipes containing all-purpose or bread flour.

However, I prefer to make my gluten-free dough with mashed cauliflower. Once thickened with egg and flavored with cheese, this mixture is spread on a baking sheet and par-baked into a slightly springy crust. True, nobody is going to confuse this with a flour-containing crust, but it is simple to make and delicious in its own right.

MAKES ONE 10-INCH PIE

1 large head of cauliflower, chopped (use all of the cauliflower, including the stems)

85 grams (3 ounces) grated aged provolone

1 large egg

Fine sea salt, pepper, and other seasonings

1. Preheat your Baking Steel in the oven at 450°F for 45 minutes. Unlike some of our other pizza recipes, this one is not going for full-throttle heat.

2. Place the chopped cauliflower in the bowl of a food processor; pulverize until the mixture resembles mashed potatoes.

3. Transfer the mixture to a microwave-safe bowl and heat for 5 minutes on high. Remove, spread the mixture on a clean tea towel, and let cool. Then gather all four corners of the towel, fold them over the cauliflower, and squeeze out the excess liquid.

4. Place the cauliflower in a large bowl and add the cheese, egg, salt and pepper, and other seasonings to taste. Stir until the mixture comes together to form a dough.

5. Spread the mixture on parchment paper and form it into a circle approximately 10 inches wide.

6. Launch the parchment paper with the gluten-free dough onto your preheated steel and bake for 10 to 12 minutes or until slightly dry in appearance. Without turning off the oven, remove the dough (still on the parchment) from the steel using your peel and transfer it to a heat-safe surface.

7. While the par-baked crust is still hot, top it with the toppings of your choice (I like a traditional tomato sauce and a duo of cheeses: low-moisture mozzarella and aged provolone). Then relaunch the topped crust, still on the sheet of parchment paper, and bake for 5 to 6 minutes more, or until the cheese is nice and gooey and browned to your liking. Remove, slice, and serve.

THIN-CRUST PIZZA DOUGH

When it comes to crust, everyone has an opinion. For some, the heftier the better; even Sicilian crust isn't thick enough. Others prefer a chewy crust like a New York slice. And for still others, it's only real pizza if it has a cracker-thin, crispy crust. If you're a member of the "thin is in" camp, this crust is for you.

The secret to its success? First, you'll use less dough per serving; the dough-ball portions weigh in at around 140 grams each, or about 40 percent smaller than our Seventy-Two-Hour Pizza Dough dough balls. Second, you'll stretch it super-thin and roll it with a rolling pin to knock out air bubbles. The thin, flatter dough attains a perfectly crispy texture when baked. Top it lightly and let the edges blister for the best results.

MAKES SIX 10-INCH PIES

500 grams (3¾ cups) bread flour

16 grams (1 tablespoon) fine sea salt

1 gram (¼ teaspoon) active dry yeast

1¼ cups water, at room temperature

1. In a large bowl, whisk together the bread flour, salt, and yeast.

2. Slowly add the water and mix with a wooden spoon just to combine. Once the mixture is moistened, remove from the bowl with lightly oiled or wet hands (to discourage sticking) and knead on a lightly floured work surface for 2 to 3 minutes to remove any clumps. The dough won't become elastic but should easily form a loose ball.

3. Place the dough in a lightly oiled bowl and cover with a damp, clean kitchen towel or plastic wrap.

4. Place on the counter for 24 hours at room temperature. The dough will double in size and you may see bubbles forming on the surface.

5. Lightly flour a large cutting board or your countertop and turn the dough out onto it. Wet or lightly oil your hands again.

6. Divide dough into 6 equal portions (about 140 grams each). Form the dough into balls.

7. Place each dough portion in a lightly oiled, airtight container; label with the date. Refrigerate for up to 5 days.

8. Remove the dough from the refrigerator 1 hour before using to allow it to come to room temperature.

9. To roll out the dough, place it on a lightly floured work surface and punch it down into a circle roughly 5 inches in diameter. Then, using a rolling pin, roll it horizontally and vertically to work it into a circle about ⅛ inch thick and 11 to 12 inches across. Knock out any additional air bubbles by hand to ensure the dough stays flat as it cooks.

BAR PIZZA DOUGH

Bar pizza is a delicious Massachusetts creation. It's not the type of thing you'll see in a high-end restaurant or even at a by-the-slice joint; it's most at home in dimly lit dive bars.

It's definitely not health food—this pizza dough is cooked in a pan that's saturated with olive oil. The fairly thin dough absorbs the oil and crisps on the bottom, so every bite is full of flavor. Because we give this dough so little time to ferment, it's extremely wet and sticky, and it's best to let a stand mixer do the kneading for you. Paired with a cold beer, pizza with this crust offers a true taste of old-school Boston.

MAKES FOUR 10-INCH PIES

550 grams (4½ cups) all-purpose flour

21 grams (1 tablespoon plus 1 teaspoon) fine sea salt

1 gram (¼ teaspoon) active dry yeast

1½ cups water, warm (about 105°F)

1 tablespoon olive oil

1. Sift the dry ingredients into the bowl of a stand mixer fitted with the dough-hook attachment.

2. Add the warm water and mix for 2 minutes on low. Add the olive oil and mix until the dough starts to look smooth and a bit shiny and pulls away from the sides of the bowl, about 2 minutes more.

3. Let the dough rest for 20 minutes, then place it in a bowl and let it rest for 2 hours or until dough has doubled in size.

4. Lightly flour your work surface and remove mixture. Divide dough into 4 equal portions.

5. Let the dough proof for 2 hours on a lightly floured sheet tray, covered with plastic, before proceeding with the recipe (page 86).

I WANT PIZZA TONIGHT DOUGH

It's all well and good to create hand-crafted pizza dough that has been allowed forty-eight hours to ferment for optimum flavor. But what are you having for dinner tonight?

For those times when you can't start the dough days in advance, here's a recipe that you can make the same day, though you do still need a few hours for the dough to rise. It might lack the complex flavor of Seventy-Two-Hour Pizza Dough, but it will yield a fresh, homemade dough that tastes way better than takeout. Unfortunately, pizza dough that isn't given at least a little time to rise just isn't very good, so we don't recommend making this unless you have at least an hour to prepare it.

MAKES FOUR 10-INCH PIES OR THREE 12- TO 14-INCH PIES

500 grams (3¾ cups) bread flour

16 grams (1 tablespoon) fine sea salt

1 gram (¼ teaspoon) active dry yeast

1½ cups water, warm (about 105°F)

1. In a large bowl, whisk together the flour, salt, and yeast.

2. Slowly add the water and mix with a wooden spoon just to combine.

3. Once the mixture is moistened, remove from the bowl with lightly oiled or wet hands and knead on a lightly floured work surface for 2 to 3 minutes to remove any clumps.

4. Place the dough in a lightly oiled bowl and cover with a damp, clean kitchen towel or plastic wrap. Let rest on the countertop for 30 minutes.

5. Lightly flour a large cutting board or countertop and turn the dough out onto it. Knead the dough again for 2 minutes until elastic and stretchy. Place the dough back in the bowl, cover with plastic wrap or a clean, damp kitchen towel, and let proof for 2 hours or until doubled in size.

6. Turn the dough back out onto your lightly floured work surface. Divide into 3 or 4 equal portions, depending on the size of the pizza you're making.

7. Form each portion into a ball, then wrap each ball in plastic wrap and let rest at room temperature for an hour or two for optimal flavor and texture.

8. After the resting period, you're ready to roll; it's time to make pizza!

LEFTOVERS If you're using only a portion of this dough, you can save the rest for later use. Simply place in a lightly oiled container and store in the refrigerator for up to a week. As an added benefit, the flavors will intensify after a day or two, making something similar to the Seventy-Two-Hour Pizza Dough.

CHICAGO-STYLE DEEP-DISH PIZZA DOUGH

This dough truly puts the *pie* in *pizza pie*. It's traditional to include butter in Chicago-style deep-dish pizza dough; this gives the crust a rich flavor and a tender texture on the inside and crispy, nicely browned edges on the outside. It's one of those things that you simply must taste to believe.

MAKES ONE 12-INCH CHICAGO-STYLE DEEP-DISH PIZZA

450 grams (3⅔ cups) all-purpose flour

22 grams (2 tablespoons) cornmeal

16 grams (1 tablespoon) fine sea salt

2 grams (½ teaspoon) active dry yeast

2 tablespoons olive oil

4 tablespoons unsalted butter, melted

1 cup water, warm (about 105°F)

1. In a large bowl, whisk together the flour, cornmeal, salt, and yeast.

2. In a separate medium bowl, combine the olive oil, melted butter, and water, and stir to combine.

3. Slowly pour the wet ingredients into the dry ingredients and mix with a wooden spoon until well combined and the mixture comes together to form a loose dough.

4. With lightly oiled or wet hands, turn the dough out onto a well-floured work surface. Knead by hand for 2 to 3 minutes until the dough comes together. Form into a ball.

5. Place the dough in an oiled bowl, cover with a damp, clean kitchen towel or plastic wrap, and let rest for 24 hours at room temperature. It will double in size and you may see bubbles forming on the surface.

6. Lightly flour a large cutting board or countertop and turn the dough out onto it. Wet or lightly oil your hands again.

7. Shape the dough into a ball. Place the ball in a well-oiled 12-inch-round straight-sided baking pan. Cover with lightly oiled plastic wrap and let rest for 2 hours before proceeding with the recipe (page 92).

SAUCES

Sauce may be the most overlooked part of the pizza trifecta (of sauce, crust, and toppings). Yet it's what enables the flavors on top and underneath to shine. I take a minimalist approach to sauce, focusing on good quality and simple ingredients. They do their work quietly and help make your pizzas perfect.

NO-COOK TOMATO SAUCE

Less is more—the key to our favorite tomato sauce is doing as little as possible and letting the tomatoes steal the show.

I love the rich flavor that comes from good canned crushed tomatoes; I strain them, add fine sea salt, and voilà—tomato sauce! This simple sauce will give your pizza a classic flavor. Since it will heat naturally on top of your pie, you don't need to warm up the sauce beforehand.

If you've got some fresh, ripe plum tomatoes nearby, simply crush them by hand or pulse them in a food processor or blender, add salt, and proceed.

MAKES ABOUT 4 CUPS
(ENOUGH FOR SEVEN OR EIGHT 12-INCH PIZZAS)

1 (28-ounce) can crushed tomatoes

Fine sea salt

If using a food processor or blender: Pour the contents of the can into the bowl of a food processor or strong blender (you can strain it if you like; I don't bother anymore). Add salt to taste. Pulse a few times, just to mix everything up and get the tomato chunks dispersed in the juice.

If working by hand: Strain the tomatoes, discard the excess liquid, and pour them into a large bowl. Use your hands to tear and crush the tomatoes until you've attained a texture you like for sauce. Add salt to taste.

VARIATIONS For more flavor, add a couple of cloves of thinly sliced garlic, a teaspoon of chopped fresh oregano, or any other aromatics and spices you like.

When you spread the sauce on your dough, you always leave some space around the perimeter of the pie. This gives you a non-sauce-covered crust to hold on to and prevents sauce from sloshing over the sides. If you do have a spill, simply remove the excess sauce from the peel and toss down some bread flour or semolina to absorb the remaining moisture.

But how much room do you need to leave? I suggest one inch in my recipes, but you can feel free to experiment depending on how much crust you like. In general, the sauce will spread out slightly with the weight of the toppings.

●

PERFECT PESTO

Every year around August, I find my refrigerator packed with an excess of basil. While it's a pleasant enough problem to have, it can be tricky to figure out a way to use it all while it's in peak form. My favorite solution? I make a big batch of pesto sauce. This pesto, inspired by my friend Alexandra Stafford, blogger at *Alexandra's Kitchen*, imparts a powerful flavor to pizza and tastes just as great with pasta or spread on sandwiches.

MAKES ENOUGH FOR ONE 12-INCH PIZZA

225 grams (about 1 cup loosely packed) basil leaves

25 to 40 grams (2 small cloves) garlic, minced

Pinch of fine sea salt

Crushed red pepper flakes

50 grams (2 tablespoons) finely grated Parmigiano-Reggiano or Pecorino Romano

2 to 3 tablespoons olive oil

1. On a cutting board, chiffonade the basil by stacking the basil leaves, rolling them into a cylinder (as you would a yoga mat), and cutting into thin slices using a chef's knife. Then mince the slices.

2. In a small bowl, combine the garlic and basil. Season with a pinch of salt, a pinch of crushed red pepper flakes, and the grated cheese. Add 2 to 3 tablespoons of olive oil (just enough to submerge the dry ingredients). Stir to combine. This sauce is best used immediately but can be stored in an airtight container in the fridge for up to 3 days. It may turn slightly brown, but it will still taste great.

ROASTED GARLIC AND GARLIC OIL

Roasted garlic is a magical ingredient that lends flavor to everything. This recipe is perfect for pizza toppings, but you might just find yourself adding it to mashed potatoes, pasta dishes, stir-fry creations...the list goes on. When you make your own roasted garlic, you get a two-for-one special: the garlic itself, and the oil it cooked in. The oil is just as magical as the garlic and imparts deliciousness to everything it touches.

MAKES ½ CUP

1 head of garlic

¾ cup canola oil

4 tablespoons olive oil

1. Position a rack in the middle of your oven. Preheat the oven for 15 minutes at 350°F. You don't need to use your Baking Steel for this recipe, but it certainly won't hurt to have it in there.

2. Peel a head of garlic into cloves. Place in a roasting dish and cover with the canola and olive oils.

3. Roast in the preheated oven until the garlic is golden brown. Strain out the garlic and save the oil. Now you have garlic oil; you're welcome! Store the roasted garlic for 4 to 5 days in the fridge; the garlic oil will keep for up to 6 months.

PIZZA RECIPES

The crust and the sauce are part of the story of pizza, but what's on top makes the pie. From the classics to creative specialty pies, these recipes will help you paint your crust canvas perfectly so that every meal is a masterpiece.

In general, let the recipe measurements for ingredients serve as a loose guide. If you like more cheese or less sauce or you want to lighten up or load up on toppings, this is *your* adventure.

America's Most Popular Pizza Toppings

1. Pepperoni
2. Mushrooms
3. Onions
4. Sausages
5. Bacon
6. Extra cheese
7. Black olives
8. Green peppers
9. Pineapple
10. Spinach

What's your favorite pizza topping? If you said, "Pepperoni," you've got a lot of company; turns out, the salty thin-sliced meat is America's most popular pizza topping, even beating out extra cheese. Here are the top ten pizza toppings as identified by Foodler.com.

MARGHERITA PIZZA

Margherita is not a plain cheese pizza but rather a simple pie topped with tomato sauce, mozzarella, basil, olive oil, salt, and pepper. Each flavor works in harmony with the others to make the ultimate pizza experience.

This is a killer version of a classic Margherita: Seventy-Two-Hour Pizza Dough, No-Cook Tomato Sauce, fresh whole-milk mozzarella, and fresh-picked basil. Simple, yes, but a recipe for success.

A Margherita can act as the template for many other pizzas; you can omit the basil (as in the photograph on the facing page) and add sausage, pepperoni, tomatoes—whatever you can dream up!

MAKES ONE 12-INCH PIZZA

1 ball Seventy-Two-Hour Pizza Dough or your favorite pizza dough

Flour for dusting

¼ cup No-Cook Tomato Sauce (page 48)

150 grams (about 5 ounces) fresh mozzarella, thinly sliced or torn by hand

4 to 5 leaves fresh basil

Olive oil

Fine sea salt and pepper

1. Preheat the Baking Steel in your oven (page 19).

2. Stretch your dough into a 12-inch circle (oblong or oval is also fine). Lightly flour your peel and place the dough on top.

3. Set the oven to Broil.

4. Evenly distribute the tomato sauce across the top of the pizza, leaving about 1 inch around the perimeter for the crust.

5. Place mozzarella evenly atop the sauced surface. Less is more; it will ooze in the oven's heat. Add half the basil leaves on top.

6. Use a generously floured pizza peel to launch your pizza onto the Baking Steel and bake under the broiler for 2 minutes.

7. After 2 minutes, open the oven and use your pizza peel to give the pizza a 180-degree turn. Turn off the broiler, set the oven to its highest temperature, and continue cooking for another 1 to 2 minutes or until the cheese has attained the desired brownness.

8. Use your pizza peel to remove the pie from the oven. Top with the remaining basil. Finish with a drizzle of olive oil and salt and pepper to taste. Slice and serve.

FOUR-CHEESE PIZZA (WHITE PIZZA)

If you think the best part of a pizza is the cheese, this is the pie for you. This pizza avoids any mention of sauce and replaces it with cheese and more cheese plus a sprinkling of red pepper flakes—you know, for contrast.

You'll start with hand-torn mozzarella, which will add a creamy flavor. Then you'll fill in the gaps with provolone and fontina, which will add richness and an intense goo factor. After you bake, go ahead and add some Parmigiano-Reggiano, and use a heavy hand. Amazingly, this white pizza ends up light in spite of its heavy topping, and it's so damn tasty you may not want to share.

MAKES ONE 12-INCH PIZZA

1 ball Seventy-Two-Hour Pizza Dough or your favorite pizza dough

Flour for dusting

150 grams (about 5 ounces) fresh mozzarella, torn or thinly sliced

50 grams (2 ounces) aged provolone, grated

50 grams (2 ounces) fontina, grated

10 grams (1 teaspoon) crushed red pepper flakes

25 grams (½ ounce) Parmigiano-Reggiano

Garlic oil

1. Preheat the Baking Steel in your oven (page 19).

2. Stretch your dough into a 12-inch circle (oblong or oval is also fine). Lightly flour your peel and place the dough on top.

3. Set the oven to Broil.

4. Evenly distribute the mozzarella, provolone, and fontina on top of the dough, leaving about an inch around the perimeter for the crust. Sprinkle the pepper flakes evenly on top.

5. Use a generously floured pizza peel to launch your pizza onto the Baking Steel and bake under the broiler for 2 minutes.

6. After 2 minutes, open the oven and use your pizza peel to give the pizza a 180-degree turn. Turn off the broiler, set the oven to its highest temperature, and continue cooking for another 1 to 2 minutes or until the cheese has attained the desired brownness.

7. Use your pizza peel to remove the pie from the oven. Grate Parmigiano-Reggiano on top and drizzle with garlic oil. Slice and serve.

FUNGHI (FUN-GUY) PIZZA

There are hundreds, even thousands of wild-mushroom varieties out there. We chose shiitake, oyster, and cremini, all of which you'll be able to find at your local grocery store. Coat the mushrooms in a little olive oil, salt, and pepper, and let them cook on top of the pizza in the oven. Using that dry heat from the broiler gives these *funghi* a superb texture.

Here's an easy way to get everyone in a pizza-party mood: Start to make a Funghi Pizza, and while you're doing that, come up with as many bad puns related to "fun-guy" as humanly possible. The pizza should be ready by the time your guests are about to run out of your house, and all will be forgiven.

No exotic mushrooms to be found? White button mushrooms will work too. They won't be quite as complex, but they'll still make a fine pie.

MAKES ONE 12-INCH PIZZA

1 ball Seventy-Two-Hour Pizza Dough or your favorite pizza dough

Flour for dusting

75 grams (3 ounces) Taleggio, thinly sliced

25 to 30 grams (1 ounce) fresh mozzarella, torn

Olive oil

75 grams (3 ounces) mixed wild mushrooms, thinly sliced and tossed in olive oil and fine sea salt

10 grams (about 1 clove) garlic, thinly sliced

25 grams (1 ounce) basil, chiffonaded (page 67)

1. Preheat the Baking Steel in your oven (page 19).

2. Stretch your dough into a 12-inch circle (oblong or oval is also fine). Lightly flour your peel and place the dough on top.

3. Set the oven to Broil.

4. Distribute the Taleggio and mozzarella evenly across the top of the pizza, leaving about 1 inch around the perimeter for the crust. Give the whole thing a healthy drizzle of olive oil.

5. Spread your wild mushrooms across the pizza. Don't be afraid to reach the very rim of the crust with these; it makes the finished pie look interesting. Top with the garlic slices and basil.

6. Use a generously floured pizza peel to launch your pizza onto the Baking Steel, and bake under the broiler for 2 minutes.

7. After 2 minutes, open the oven and use your pizza peel to give the pizza a 180-degree turn. Turn off the broiler, set the oven to its highest temperature, and continue cooking for another 1 to 2 minutes or until the cheese has attained the desired brownness.

8. Use your pizza peel to remove the pie from the oven. Slice and serve.

NAKED PESTO PIZZA

You know summer has arrived when a regular cheese slice at your favorite pizzeria all of a sudden seems too cheesy, too greasy, too heavy. In an effort to make a lightened-up version of a favorite pizza, I stripped it of its cheeses and baked the dough naked. Unburdened by layers of toppings, the dough baked up with a perfect spring and a craggy texture pocked with crests and craters—the ideal topography to capture a heavy brushing of herb-and-garlic olive oil.

The beauty is in the simplicity; simply bake the dough, brush with herb-and-garlic olive oil, and top with the pesto mixture. It's also very easy to adapt this recipe to suit your taste and ingredient availability; change up the herbs, add some spices, throw in some nuts. Blogger and Baking Steel fan Alexandra Stafford, who writes the blog *Alexandra's Kitchen*, tops her pizza with a bunch of fresh greens. Whatever you do to it, this herb-covered naked pizza makes an irresistible summer appetizer or an excellent complement to a hearty salad.

MAKES ONE 12-INCH PIZZA

1 ball Seventy-Two-Hour Pizza Dough or your favorite pizza dough

Flour for dusting

Olive oil

3 or 4 ice cubes (see sidebar)

1 batch Perfect Pesto (page 50)

Fine sea salt

1. Preheat the Baking Steel in your oven (page 19).

2. Stretch your dough into a 12-inch circle (oblong or oval is also fine). Lightly flour your peel and place the dough on top.

3. Drizzle the dough lightly with olive oil and place 3 or 4 ice cubes in the center of the dough.

4. Use a generously floured pizza peel to launch your pizza onto the Baking Steel and bake under the broiler for 2 minutes.

5. After 2 minutes, open the oven and use your pizza peel to give the pizza a 180-degree turn. Turn off the broiler, set the oven to its highest temperature, and continue cooking for another 1 to 2 minutes or until the crust has reached the desired brownness.

6. Use your pizza peel to remove the pie from the oven. Working with the pizza still on the peel, spread the pesto evenly on top and sprinkle with salt to taste. Slice and serve.

Need Some Ice for That Burn?

What do ice cubes have to do with getting naked?

No, things didn't just get weird. I'm talking about a cool method I picked up to create the perfect crust on naked (that is, baked-before-it's-topped) pizza. Usually, when you bake a naked pizza using the broiler, the dough burns, which doesn't make for a pretty pizza. However, things change when you add a little ice. Simply put a couple of ice cubes in the center of the dough before launching, and you'll see two key benefits: the added moisture will keep the dough moist in the center, and the ice will prevent the crust from burning. It's genius! Give it a try the next time you're baking naked.

HOT HAWAIIAN ISLAND PIZZA

The so-called Hawaiian pizza was actually conceived by Sam Panopoulos, a proud Canadian with no particular ties to the Aloha State. Its ingredients have a distinct Hawaiian flair, though; generous amounts of pineapple and ham top the tomato-sauce-and-cheese base. It's become a pizza classic in America, but its popularity in the United States is nothing compared to how much it's loved in Australia. There, it is by far the most popular pizza, accounting for 15 percent of all pizza sales.

But even though Hawaiian pizza is now a standard, there's nothing traditional about it, so I don't feel bad about getting creative with its construction.

I jokingly call this pie PB and J, but don't worry, there's no peanut butter (or jelly) in it. Here, PB and J means pineapple, bacon, and jalapeño, and it packs a lot of heat. The heat of the Baking Steel means you don't have to precook your bacon; it crisps up fine in the oven.

MAKES ONE 12-INCH PIZZA

1 ball Seventy-Two-Hour Pizza Dough	50 grams (2 ounces) fontina, shredded
Flour for dusting	110 grams (½ cup) cubed or diced pineapple
¼ cup tomato sauce	1 small jalapeño, thinly sliced
50 grams (2 ounces) fresh mozzarella, torn	3 strips bacon, uncooked

1. Preheat the Baking Steel in your oven (page 19).

2. Stretch your dough into a 12-inch circle (oblong or oval is also fine). Lightly flour your peel and place the dough on top.

3. Set the oven to Broil.

4. Evenly distribute the tomato sauce across the top of the pizza, leaving about 1 inch around perimeter for the crust.

5. Evenly sprinkle the cheeses over the sauce. Top with the rest of the ingredients, trying to evenly distribute the pineapple, jalapeño, and raw bacon.

6. Use a generously floured pizza peel to launch your pizza onto the Baking Steel and bake under the broiler for 2 minutes.

7. After 2 minutes, open the oven and use your pizza peel to give the pizza a 180-degree turn. Turn off the broiler, set the oven to its highest temperature, and continue cooking for another 1 to 2 minutes or until the cheese has attained the desired brownness.

8. Use your pizza peel to remove the pie from the oven. Slice and serve.

ALLIUM PIZZA

Did you know that in Indiana, it's illegal to attend a public event or use public transportation within four hours of eating onions or garlic? If you're in the Hoosier State, prepare to hunker down for the next few hours, because this allium (the fancy-pants term for onions and aromatics) pizza is packed with two types of onions and leeks for good measure. Elsewhere in the world, you'll be free to travel as you please, but for everyone's safety, please invest in mints.

Break out the goggles or prepare to cry it out while prepping this pizza; chopping all those onions and leeks may make you shed a tear or ten. But they'll turn into tears of joy once you take your first bite, because flavor seekers will find that this allium-packed pie is pure pungent pizza perfection.

MAKES ONE 12-INCH PIZZA

1 ball Seventy-Two-Hour Pizza Dough or your favorite pizza dough

Flour for dusting

75 grams (3 ounces) fontina, sliced

50 grams (about ¼ cup) caramelized onions (recipe follows)

50 grams (about ¼ cup) chopped leeks

50 grams (about ¼ cup) thinly sliced red onion

12 grams (1 tablespoon) chopped chives

25 grams (1 ounce) Parmigiano-Reggiano

1. Preheat the Baking Steel in your oven (page 19).

2. Stretch your dough into a 12-inch circle (oblong or oval is also fine). Lightly flour your peel and place the dough on top.

3. Set the oven to Broil.

4. Spread the fontina evenly on top of the pizza, leaving about 1 inch around the perimeter for the crust. Scatter the caramelized onions, leeks, and red onion evenly across the top.

5. Use a generously floured pizza peel to launch your pizza onto the Baking Steel and bake under the broiler for 2 minutes.

6. After 2 minutes, open the oven and use your pizza peel to give the pizza a 180-degree turn. Turn off the broiler, set the oven to its highest temperature, and continue cooking for another 1 to 2 minutes or until the cheese has attained the desired brownness.

7. Use your pizza peel to remove the pie from the oven. Sprinkle with chopped chives and grate the Parmigiano-Reggiano on top. Slice and serve.

CARAMELIZED ONIONS

This basic recipe for caramelized onions is perfectly suited for this pie, but you might find yourself making them to top burgers, sandwiches, soups, and salads too.

4 tablespoons olive oil

1 medium-size onion, sliced thin

5 grams (1 teaspoon) fine sea salt

1. In a medium sauté pan or on your Baking Steel Griddle, heat the oil on medium heat until it begins to shimmer but is not smoking. Add the sliced onions and reduce heat to low.

2. Cook over low heat for 30 minutes, continuously stirring the onions. Continue to cook until the onions have caramelized or turned golden brown. Stir in the salt and remove from heat. If you're not using them right away, store for up to 1 week in an airtight container in the refrigerator.

MEAT LOVER'S PIZZA

Vegetarians, avert your eyes; this pizza is unabashedly a meat lover's delight. A basic cheese pizza is transformed into a carnivore's dream, topped with a mixture of beef, pepperoni, bacon, and chorizo. As the meats bake, their flavors not only meld together but infuse the cheese and sauce. The pie is kissed with a touch of onion and basil for an extra punch of pungency.

This is a hearty and satisfying pizza and is especially good alongside a cold beer. Make it for your next party or to really wow the crowd on game day.

MAKES ONE 12-INCH PIZZA

1 ball Seventy-Two-Hour Pizza Dough or your favorite pizza dough

Flour for dusting

¼ cup tomato sauce

25 grams (1 ounce) ground beef (we prefer 85 percent lean)

25 grams (1 ounce) pepperoni, thinly sliced

1 strip bacon, cut into small pieces

25 grams (1 ounce) cured chorizo, thinly sliced

75 grams (3 ounces) fontina, shredded

50 grams (2 ounces) fresh mozzarella, torn or thinly sliced

50 grams (2 ounces) chopped white onions

25 grams (1 ounce) fresh basil, thinly sliced (see note)

1. Preheat the Baking Steel in your oven (page 19).

2. Stretch your dough into a 12-inch circle (oblong or oval is also fine). Lightly flour your peel and place the dough on top.

3. Set the oven to Broil.

4. Evenly distribute the tomato sauce across the top of the pizza, leaving about 1 inch around perimeter for the crust.

5. Evenly distribute the meats and the cheeses across the pizza, then scatter the onions on top.

6. Use a generously floured pizza peel to launch your pizza onto the Baking Steel and bake under the broiler for 2 minutes.

7. After 2 minutes, open the oven and use your pizza peel to give the pizza a 180-degree turn. Turn off the broiler, set the oven to its highest temperature, and continue cooking for another 1 to 2 minutes or until the cheese has attained the desired brownness.

8. Use your pizza peel to remove the pie from the oven. Top with the basil. Slice and serve.

EXTRA CREDIT Slicing herbs? One of the most efficient ways to slice delicate leaves like basil is the chiffonade, which is a fancy term for grabbing a bunch of leaves, stacking them neatly on top of one another, and slicing. I like to grab seven or eight leaves, stack them, and roll them up like you would a yoga mat. Then I slice perpendicular to the roll, and voilà! Even strips of greens.

CHORIZO WITH FONTINA AND MOZZARELLA PIZZA

For many, sausage on pizza instantly equals Italian-style sausage. But I'd like to offer something different: chorizo, a spicy pork and paprika sausage that cooks beautifully at high temperatures. Chorizo loves cheese, and it joins in a ménage à trois with a mélange of mozzarella and nutty fontina, which act as the perfect complement to the sausage's spiciness. Finished with a few sprigs of parsley for flavor (and for something green), this pizza is easy to make and has a refined taste that is hard to find in a sausage pie.

MAKES ONE 12-INCH PIZZA

1 ball Seventy-Two-Hour Pizza Dough

Flour for dusting

¼ cup No-Cook Tomato Sauce (page 48)

75 grams (about 2½ ounces) fresh mozzarella, torn

75 grams (about 2½ ounces) fontina, shredded

75 grams (2½ ounces) cured chorizo, thinly sliced

15 grams (1 tablespoon) finely chopped parsley

1. Preheat the Baking Steel in your oven (page 19).

2. Stretch your dough into a 12-inch circle (oblong or oval is also fine). Lightly flour your peel and place the dough on top.

3. Set the oven to Broil.

4. Evenly distribute the sauce and cheeses across the top of the pizza, leaving about 1 inch around the perimeter for the crust. Layer the chorizo on top.

5. Use a generously floured pizza peel to launch your pizza onto the Baking Steel and bake under the broiler for 2 minutes.

CONT.

6. After 2 minutes, open the oven and use your pizza peel to give the pizza a 180-degree turn. Turn off the broiler, set the oven to its highest temperature, and continue cooking for another 1 to 2 minutes or until the cheese has attained the desired brownness. Use a peel to remove from oven. Sprinkle with the parsley, slice, and serve.

NOTE **One of my favorite ways** to finish this pie is with a product I recently discovered called Mike's Hot Honey. Made in Brooklyn, this chili pepper–infused honey is almost alarmingly addictive and brings a great heat to this flavorful pie. Drizzle it on directly after baking.

Sausage Debate: In Praise of *Not* Cooking Sausage Before Putting It on Your Pie

There was a time when I would cook my sausage, or at least par-cook it, before putting it on pizza. Those days are over, and I'd like to make a case for not cooking your sausage before putting it on your pie.

The fear of serving partially raw sausage to your guests is really unfounded when you're cooking with the Baking Steel. Since you're combining the broiler method with the high temperature of the steel itself, the sausage will have no trouble cooking through, and since you're not transferring the sausages from another pan, their juices will seep into the pizza, giving it a full and unbelievably delicious flavor. As an added bonus, less cooking will yield a more tender texture—no chewy, rubbery, overcooked sausage here.

The only potential downfall of not precooking your sausage is that it never attains the perfect browning at the same time as the cheese does. Happily, Kenji López-Alt has provided a solution for that. Before putting the sausage pieces on your pizza, gently roll them in flour and then tap off the excess. This will promote more rapid browning so the sausage will have a perfect crust on top.

ARUGULA WITH CARAMELIZED ONIONS AND BALSAMIC PIZZA

This pizza holds the honor of being my wife's absolute favorite. While it's a worthy pizza any time of year, it truly shines in early July, when the first fresh arugula is coming out of the ground. The stuff you buy at the grocery store (even the good kind) doesn't come close to the addictively astringent, thoroughly green, zingy flavor of the farm-fresh variety.

When you combine the arugula with fontina cheese, sweet caramelized onions, and a splash of balsamic vinegar, you get a pie that has just enough going on. It's an elegant pizza that tastes fancy but is very easy to make. So keep an eye on the offerings at your local farmers' market and really knock your friends' socks off with this one.

MAKES ONE 12-INCH PIZZA

1 ball Seventy-Two-Hour Pizza Dough or your favorite pizza dough

Flour for dusting

100 grams (4 ounces) fontina, thinly sliced

100 grams (¼ cup) Caramelized Onions (page 65)

30 grams (about 1 cup loosely packed) arugula

1 tablespoon balsamic vinegar

Fine sea salt

1. Preheat the Baking Steel in your oven (page 19).

2. Stretch your dough into a 12-inch circle (oblong or oval is also fine). Lightly flour your peel and place the dough on top.

3. Set the oven to Broil.

4. Evenly distribute the fontina and Caramelized Onions across the top of the pizza, leaving about 1 inch around the perimeter for the crust.

5. Use a generously floured pizza peel to launch your pizza onto the Baking Steel and bake under the broiler for 2 minutes.

6. After 2 minutes, open the oven and use your pizza peel to give the pizza a 180-degree turn. Turn off the broiler, set the oven to its highest temperature, and continue cooking for another 1 to 2 minutes or until the cheese has attained the desired brownness.

7. Use your pizza peel to remove the pie from the oven. Scatter the arugula over the top. Splash with balsamic vinegar and then sprinkle with salt to taste. Slice and serve.

SOUS-VIDE-EGG AND BACON PIZZA

"Put an egg on it" has become something of a culinary cliché. But clichés exist for a reason, and I am telling you, putting an egg on your pizza is worth your time.

But there's an art to delivering pizza hot and with an oozing yolk on top, and my early attempts weren't promising. Most of the time, the egg was overcooked. Partially baking the dough first didn't help; in some cases, I overcooked the dough, and in others, my over-easy eggs turned out hard-boiled!

Redemption came by way of an immersion circulator (readily available online; I like the ones made by Sansaire and Anova Culinary), a one-stop appliance for all your sous-vide needs. Sous vide (pronounced "sue-veed" in your Frenchiest accent) is a method of cooking food in a temperature-controlled water bath. After preparing an egg sous vide–style, I simply cracked it on top of my finished pizza for a reliably oozing yolk every time.

While it's possible to prepare food sous vide without serious machinery, once you start using this method, you'll become addicted to the flavor and quality, so you might decide that it's well worth shelling out a few hundred bucks for an immersion circulator. (I make sous-vide eggs almost weekly.) If you don't want them on your pizza, try them on toast!

MAKES ONE 12-INCH PIZZA

1 ball Seventy-Two-Hour Pizza Dough or your favorite pizza dough

Flour for dusting

100 grams (4 ounces) fresh mozzarella, torn

3 or 4 slices bacon, uncooked

1 or 2 sous-vide or poached eggs (see page 76)

Fine sea salt and pepper

15 grams (1 tablespoon) chopped parsley

1. Preheat the Baking Steel in your oven (page 19).

2. Stretch your dough into a 12-inch circle (oblong or oval is also fine). Lightly flour your peel and place the dough on top.

3. Set the oven to Broil.

4. Evenly distribute the mozzarella and bacon across the top of the pizza, leaving about 1 inch around the perimeter for the crust.

5. Use a generously floured pizza peel to launch your pizza onto the Baking Steel and bake under the broiler for 2 minutes.

6. After 2 minutes, open the oven and use your pizza peel to give the pizza a 180-degree turn. Turn off the broiler, set the oven to its highest temperature, and continue

cooking for another 1 to 2 minutes or until the bacon is cooked and the cheese has attained the desired brownness.

7. Use your pizza peel to remove the pie from the oven. Crack your sous-vide eggs into a bowl and drain any excess liquid with a fine-mesh strainer. Place the eggs on top of your pizza and season with sea salt and pepper to taste. Sprinkle chopped parsley over the whole thing. Slice and serve.

SOUS-VIDE EGGS

This easy method will work with most immersion circulators.

1. Set your immersion circulator to 64°C (147°F).

2. Once the water has heated, use a spoon to carefully place the eggs in the water bath.

3. Allow eggs to cook in the water bath for 20 minutes. After 20 minutes in the water bath, remove the eggs and shock them with cold water to stop the cooking process. Once they're cool enough to touch, you can use the eggs immediately or store in the fridge until ready to use. They'll keep for 4 to 5 days.

NOTE **As an alternative to sous-vide eggs,** try poaching your eggs. Any cooking method will work, as long as your eggs are cooked and ready for topping ahead of time.

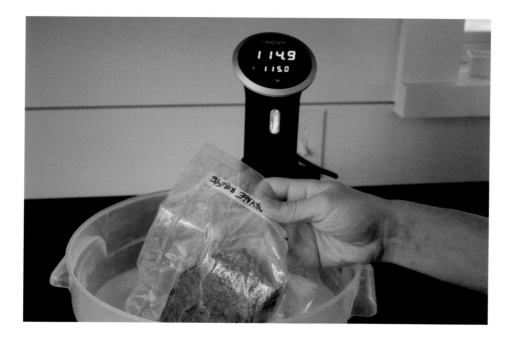

Pizzagram: Tips for Taking the Best Pizza Pictures on Instagram

People eat with their eyes first. Perhaps that's why food photos are so liked on social media. Here are my sometimes hard-earned tips for getting your pizza photos noticed on Instagram.

Natural light is absolutely best.
Ever see someone post a totally gross food pic? It was probably because of low light at a restaurant. Natural light is by far the most flattering light on food products.

Go for contrast and texture.
Pizzas featuring contrast in color and shape look best.

Take overhead shots.
Take an overhead shot of the pizza on a rustic tabletop. Boom. A winner.

Be honest.
Does it look good? Does it make you want to eat it?

Be a food stylist.
Consider how to frame the pizza in your shot. What is most dynamic, the entire pizza on the steel or a single slice on a plate? There isn't a right or wrong answer here. Do seek out good color contrast on serving vessels.

Get shots of the creamy, gooey cheese.
The gooey-cheese shots get 'em every time. For some shots, I actually slightly precooked the dough before adding the cheese so that the cheese could be captured at its gooiest point, right when the crust is browning.

Go with the classics.
You don't have to invent a fennel-banana-seaweed pizza to gain interest. Think Margherita or sausage and peppers is boring? Well, you don't have to photograph pizzas that are innovative or even creative with their toppings. People like recognizable. Pizza is a nostalgic food.

Tell a story.
Food always tastes better with a backstory. For instance, the remnants of a slice and a story about who ate it. That's interesting.

Be authentic and be real.
Yep. Be yourself. Don't try to channel Anthony Bourdain if that's not you. It will end up falling flat.

Put an egg on it.
Preferably with an oozy yolk. People love that shot of an egg on top, and you get bonus points for an oozy yolk.

Most important: Be sure to tag #bakingsteel.

FIGGY PIZZA

For many people, figs fall into the category of JFN, or "just for Newtons." If you're one of these people, it's time to expand your horizons and put figs on your next pizza. It might sound strange at first, but you'll have to believe me when I say you've got to try it. There's something about the mellow, smooth sweetness of figs that acts as a perfect complement to the rich, melty, and slightly salty cheese.

This pie embraces contrasts, with a sweet fig drizzle, mozzarella and creamy fontina, balsamic vinegar, rosemary, and arugula. The mix of sweet, creamy, earthy, and astringent makes for a pizza unlike any you've ever tasted.

MAKES ONE 12-INCH PIZZA

450 grams (1 pint) Mission figs, halved and stemmed

450 grams (1 pint) Turkish figs, halved and stemmed

⅓ cup balsamic vinegar

1 sprig fresh rosemary

1 ball Seventy-Two-Hour Pizza Dough or your favorite pizza dough

Flour for dusting

85 to 100 grams (3 to 4 ounces) fresh mozzarella, torn or thinly sliced

25 grams (1 ounce) fontina, grated

Olive oil

25 grams (about ½ cup loosely packed) fresh arugula

1. Preheat the Baking Steel in your oven (page 19).

2. Take half the Mission figs and half the Turkish figs and coarsely chop them. In a large pot, combine the chopped figs, vinegar, and sprig of rosemary. Set over medium heat and allow to lightly bubble for about 10 minutes or until thickened.

3. Transfer the mixture to a food processor or blender and puree. Allow the mixture to cool while your oven preheats.

4. Stretch your dough into a 12-inch circle (oblong or oval is also fine). Lightly flour your peel and place the dough on top.

5. Set the oven to Broil.

6. Evenly distribute the fig spread, mozzarella, and fontina across the top of the pizza, leaving about 1 inch around the perimeter for the crust. Give it a generous splash of olive oil.

7. Spread your remaining halved figs around the pizza. Don't be afraid to reach the very rim of the crust with these, as they will add visual interest to your finished pie.

8. Use a generously floured pizza peel to launch your pizza onto the Baking Steel and bake under the broiler for 2 minutes.

9. After 2 minutes, open the oven and use your pizza peel to give the pizza a 180-degree turn. Turn off the broiler, set the oven to its highest temperature, and continue cooking for another 1 to 2 minutes, or until the cheese has attained the desired brownness.

10. Use your pizza peel to remove the pie from the oven. Garnish with arugula, slice, and serve.

AVOCADO AND TOMATO PIE

Healthy pizza might sound like an oxymoron or like some flavorless product you'd find in the freezer aisle of your local grocery store. But this pizza delivers on that promise and tastes wonderful too.

It's so simple that it almost feels like a stretch to call it a recipe: Simply bake a pizza crust and then top it with mashed avocado and sliced tomatoes. Although the pie is easy to prepare, the flavor rewards are rich and complex. Every ingredient shines, and the contrast of freshly baked crust, creamy avocado with a touch of piquancy from the lime juice, and juicy tomatoes makes for a memorable dining experience. Try this one for a lighter dinner or an easy appetizer. It's good, it's healthy, and it just so happens to be vegan.

MAKES ONE 12-INCH PIZZA

1 medium avocado, mashed with a fork	Flour for dusting
Dash of lime juice	Olive oil
Fine sea salt and pepper	3 or 4 ice cubes
1 ball Thin-Crust Pizza Dough (page 42)	1 medium tomato, thinly sliced

1. Preheat the Baking Steel in your oven (page 19).

2. While the oven preheats, in a large bowl, mix your mashed avocado with a splash of lime juice (to prevent browning) and season with salt and pepper to taste.

3. Use a rolling pin to roll the pizza dough into a 12-inch circle, making sure to squish out all the bubbles. It will be fairly thin, about ⅛ inch thick, but the thin crust will lie flatter while the pizza bakes. Lightly flour your peel and carefully place the dough on top.

4. Set the oven to Broil.

5. Drizzle olive oil on top of your dough. Next, add 3 or 4 ice cubes in the center of the dough (see sidebar, page 61). Use a generously floured pizza peel to launch your pizza onto the Baking Steel and bake under the broiler for 2 minutes.

6. After 2 minutes, open the oven and use your pizza peel to give the pizza a 180-degree turn. Turn off the broiler, set the oven to its highest temperature, and continue cooking for another 1 to 2 minutes or until the crust has attained the desired brownness.

7. Use your pizza peel to remove the pie from the oven. Top with avocado mixture and tomato slices. Drizzle a bit more olive oil on top, to taste. Slice and serve.

SPICY SICILIAN PIZZA

If you're avoiding carbs, do yourself a favor and flip past this page. Inspired by the house specialty at New York City's Prince Street Pizza, this recipe is adapted from a version developed by my friend and cooking hero Kenji López-Alt, perhaps better known as the guru behind *The Food Lab*.

To make this pie, you press an entire ball of Seventy-Two-Hour Pizza Dough into a well-oiled sheet pan, then top it generously with two types of cheese, pepperoni, and tomato sauce. The crust compresses a bit under the weight of these toppings, so when it bakes up, it's a little denser than a typical pizza crust, but it's absolutely saturated with flavor; it makes for a hearty, filling slice that offers a taste of the big city. So go ahead, imagine yourself sitting on a bench on Prince Street watching the world go by as you enjoy this seriously delicious slice.

MAKES ONE 18-BY-13-INCH TRAY OF PIZZA

1 recipe Seventy-Two-Hour Pizza Dough (page 32)

Olive oil

Fine sea salt and pepper

1 cup No-Cook Tomato Sauce (page 48), spicy variation (see recipe note)

112 grams (4 ounces) fresh mozzarella, torn

112 grams (4 ounces) fontina, shredded

80 grams (3 ounces) pepperoni, thinly sliced

1. Preheat the Baking Steel in your oven (page 19).

2. Place the ball of pizza dough on a lightly oiled sheet tray. Lightly drizzle olive oil on top of the dough ball. Cover with plastic wrap (the oil will discourage sticking) and let rest for 1 hour. It will puff up slightly.

3. Remove the plastic wrap and gently press the dough until it covers the entire sheet tray. Pour a little more oil over the surface of the dough, then lightly season it with sea salt and pepper. Pour sauce over the dough, then scatter the cheese and pepperoni over the top, leaving about 1 inch around the perimeter for the crust.

4. Place the sheet tray in the oven, directly on top of the Baking Steel, and bake for 10 minutes. After 10 minutes, open the oven and rotate the sheet tray 180 degrees. Continue baking for 5 minutes or until the cheese has attained the desired brownness.

5. Using oven mitts, remove the sheet tray from the oven and let cool on top of a wire rack for 5 minutes. Cut into squares or rectangles and use a spatula to serve the slices.

NOTE **Spice up your sauce!** When making sauce for this pizza, add a pizzeria-like flavor by stirring a teaspoon of sugar, a teaspoon of fresh oregano, and a teaspoon of red pepper flakes into the mix.

How to Throw a Pizza Party

1. **Make your dough in advance.** Waiting for dough to ferment is more boring than watching paint dry, and it's excruciating for hungry guests. Do yourself (and your guests) a favor by making the dough and portioning it out in advance. Don't forget to give yourself enough time for the dough to ferment; if your pizza party is on Friday, you'll want to make the dough on Tuesday.

2. **Be smart about the type of dough you make.** Evaluate the culinary expertise of your guests. Are they foodies or are they culinary newbies with kids in tow? This can inform your decision. For newbies, Bar Pizza Dough (page 45) can be a great introduction to the world of pizza making, because you can have it stretched and ready in a pan; all your guests have to do is top it and bake. If your guests are slightly more experienced, having balls of dough ready to be stretched and topped might be a fine option.

3. **Make more dough than you think you need.** For whatever reason, people in a party mood get hungry. How many people are expected to come, and how many are kids? Planning on one and a half dough balls for each guest is usually a good bet. This allows for errors (Oops! Junior dropped a dough ball!) and for unexpected guests.

4. **Bring your dough to room temperature.** If your dough is in the fridge, let it rest at room temperature for about an hour before your guests arrive so that it will have the perfect texture for shaping and stretching. If you make it ahead and freeze it, let the dough rest for at least a few hours before your party.

5. **Preheat your oven.** Be sure to preheat the oven; nobody likes waiting an hour for the steel to heat up once a pizza is already topped. Plus, pizzas stick to the peel if they are left on it too long!

6. **Offer sauce options.** Not everyone's taste is the same. Offer more than one sauce option to suit different needs! While our basic No-Cook Tomato Sauce is a classic, you may have some who prefer it cheesy or who like it spicy. Offering spice mixes or chili flakes to flavor the tomato sauce and having a pesto sauce alternative is a good way to satisfy many different appetites.

7. **Offer toppings aplenty.** In this day and age, *toppings bar* is not only a catchphrase but a selling point. Re-create this magic in your own home by offering a cool assemblage of palate-pleasing toppings for your guests.

Cheeses

Mozzarella (fresh, aged, and smoked)	Provolone
Parmigiano-Reggiano or	Cheddar
Pecorino Romano	Ricotta
Fontina	Gouda

Meats
Pepperoni
Sausage
Bacon
Ham
Chorizo
Ground beef

Vegetables
Sliced onions
Roasted garlic
Spinach
Figs
Artichoke hearts
Mushrooms
Tomato slices
Roasted peppers
Olives or capers

For finishing
Crushed red pepper flakes
Jalapeño
Chili oil
Olive oil
Ranch dressing
Salt and pepper
Herbs and spices
Parmigiano-Reggiano
Honey

8. *Mise en place.* Make sure to prepare everything before guests arrive; grate the cheese, prep the toppings, make the sauce, caramelize the onions, slice the vegetables, roast the peppers, and put everything in its own container.

9. **Get ready.** About an hour before guests arrive, remove the dough from the fridge. Turn on the oven and place your Baking Steel on the top rack. A few minutes before people come, remove the toppings from the fridge. Have a glass of wine before guests arrive.

10. **Show 'em how it's done.** Offer a brief tutorial with some basic pizza-making tips (Don't overtop! Here's how to remedy overstretched dough!). A few pointers make for party entertainment and ensure that you won't have a big mess in your oven.

11. **Don't overdo it.** Work on a few pizzas at a time, depending on your oven setup. Do the kids' pizzas first! The parents can drink wine or beer and wait.

12. **Have your finishing materials ready.** Have a cutting board, pizza wheel, and plates ready for when the pies come out of the oven. Allow a few moments for each pizza maker to explain his or her pie; it always tastes better with a backstory.

13. **Have dessert on deck.** Having a steel chilled to make ice cream desserts is a great idea, because nothing works up an appetite like a party.

BAR PIZZA

I was born and raised in Hanover, Massachusetts, a very small community south of Boston. If you're not familiar with the area, you may not be aware that it is a high-density region for a pizza phenomenon known as bar pizza. Bar pizza isn't necessarily fancy fare; as you might expect, it's a type of pizza served at bars. But don't let that fact take away from the magic for you, because this pizza is special. On the smaller side (ten to twelve inches) and intended for one or two people, these pies have a crispy, thin crust and humble toppings. This is simple pizza done right.

The epicenter of bar-pizza tastiness, for me, is Lynwood Cafe. Located in Randolph, Massachusetts, it's about eight miles from my office. The pizza is always excellent, and I'm constantly trying—with zero luck so far—to get a glimpse in the kitchen so I can snag their pizza secrets.

I had to reverse-engineer their bar pizza, and I think we're pretty close with this recipe. The dough is typically very thin, super-crispy, and cooked well done, but not burned. Bar-pizza pans are specialized round steel pans, but you can create a similar effect by baking your pizza in a generously oiled cake pan set atop your Baking Steel. (It's oiled so that, with the help of a spatula, the pizza is easily removed.) The pie bakes for a few minutes in the pan and then is transferred directly to the Baking Steel to finish. If you want a table on a Friday night at Lynwood Cafe, you'll be waiting two to three hours; to make this pizza, all you need is about fifteen minutes (once you have the dough on hand).

MAKES ONE 12-INCH PIZZA

Olive oil

1 ball Bar Pizza Dough (page 45)

¼ cup No-Cook Tomato Sauce (page 48)

50 grams (2 ounces) of your favorite cheese blend (we use half low-moisture mozzarella, half fontina), shredded

To top (These are traditional toppings that you might see listed on the wall of a joint serving bar pizza. Stick to one of these for the authentic bar-pizza experience):

Chopped onions

Chopped green pepper

Mushrooms

Anchovies

Salami

Hamburger chunks

Pepperoni

Linguica (a garlicky Portuguese sausage)

Sausage removed from its casing

Boston baked beans

Hot peppers

Sliced meatballs

Broccoli

Barbecued chicken strips

Tomato sauce (at home, we use our No-Cook Tomato Sauce [page 48] and add dried oregano, sugar, and crushed red pepper flakes to taste)

1. Preheat the Baking Steel in your oven (page 19).

2. Generously coat the bottom of your bar-pizza or cake pan with olive oil. Stretch out your dough to make a 12-inch round. Carefully place the dough inside the pan and stretch so that the dough covers the bottom of the pan. Press the dough into the pan so that it rises about a quarter of an inch up the sides of the pan.

3. Evenly distribute tomato sauce over the surface of the dough, covering the dough all the way to the edges of the pan.

4. Sprinkle your cheese mixture evenly across the top of the pizza and top with your toppings of choice.

5. Use a pizza peel or oven mitts to launch your pan onto the Baking Steel and bake for 8 to 9 minutes. Remove the pan from the oven, carefully remove the pizza, and transfer it to a lightly floured pizza peel. Use the peel to launch the pizza directly onto your Baking Steel. Bake for 1 to 2 minutes more, until the bottom of the pizza is crisp.

DETROIT-STYLE SAUSAGE AND PEPPER PIZZA

Once a year, my wife—who is from the Detroit area—and I take a trip to Michigan, and we always make sure to eat Detroit-style pizza while we're there. This type of pie might sound odd to the uninitiated: the cheese and toppings are baked atop the crust in a special rimmed steel baking pan, and the sauce is spooned over the finished pie after baking. This means that the cheese creates a protective seal between the crust and the sauce, so the crust remains fluffy and light. The cheese is also spread all the way to the edges of the pie, which gives a tantalizing caramelized effect to the edges once baked. If you have a mandoline, use it to quickly julienne your peppers and onions.

Your Baking Steel gives your Detroit-style pizza an effect that's similar to specialized pans, which means that you'll get those perfectly crispy edges.

MAKES ONE 10-BY-14-INCH PIZZA

4 tablespoons olive oil, plus more for oiling the pan

1 ball Seventy-Two-Hour Pizza Dough or your favorite pizza dough

85 grams (½ cup) julienned green pepper

85 grams (½ cup) julienned red pepper

1 large or 2 small yellow onions, julienned

225 grams (8 ounces) uncooked Italian sausage, removed from casing and crumbled

280 grams (10 ounces) low-moisture mozzarella, diced into ¼-inch cubes

280 grams (10 ounces) fontina, diced into ¼-inch cubes

1 (14-ounce) can crushed tomatoes, strained

1 clove garlic, minced

16 grams (1 tablespoon) fine sea salt

Fine sea salt and pepper (optional)

1. Preheat the Baking Steel in your oven (page 19).

2. Generously oil a 10-by-14-inch rimmed baking sheet and place the dough ball on top. Gently roll the ball around the pan to lightly coat with oil, then cover the pan with plastic wrap. Allow to rest on the counter for 1 hour.

3. Meanwhile, in a large saucepan, combine the 4 tablespoons olive oil, peppers, and onions. Set over low heat and cook for 4 to 5 minutes or until the vegetables have softened but not yet begun to brown. Let cool.

4. Using your fingers, gently press and stretch the dough to fill the pan. When you've stretched it about as much as you can without tearing it, let the dough rest, uncovered, for about 15 minutes. Then get back in there and press and stretch the dough again, doing your best to get the dough in the corners. It's going to shrink back on you a bit, but it doesn't have to be perfect.

CONT.

5. Evenly distribute the sausage, peppers, and onions across the dough. Spread the mozzarella and fontina cubes on top, going all the way to the edges of the pan.

6. Use a pizza peel or oven mitts to launch the sheet pan on top of your Baking Steel. Bake for 14 to 16 minutes or until the cheese is browned and the edges are nice and crispy.

7. While the pizza bakes or right after it comes out of the oven, combine the crushed tomatoes, minced garlic, and salt to taste in a medium saucepan. Set over medium-low heat and keep warm until ready to serve the pizza.

8. Remove the pizza from the oven and spoon the sauce over the finished pie. Add salt and pepper if desired. Cut into rectangles and serve.

CHICAGO-STYLE DEEP-DISH PIZZA

If you've ever been to Chicago, chances are that you've sampled the deep-dish pizza, a pie that's based on the principle that if some is good, more is better. This pizza has to be baked in a pan to contain the incredible amount of cheese and sauce that tops the traditional buttery, cornmeal-flecked crust. Like its cousin the Detroit-style pizza, the deep-dish pizza needs a well-oiled pan to create the beautifully crisp crust that offers a wonderful contrast to all of the gooey toppings.

This is a pizza that truly is a pie; the crust does indeed contain butter, which gives it a pastrylike texture. The finished pizza is served in thick wedges that are oozing with cheese and totally satisfying. Even if you're normally a two- to three-slice kind of person, one slice will probably suffice here.

MAKES ONE 12-INCH DEEP-DISH PIZZA

Olive oil

1 recipe Chicago-Style Deep-Dish Pizza Dough (page 47)

For the topping

170 grams (6 ounces) mozzarella, sliced

170 grams (6 ounces) fontina, shredded

1 (28-ounce) can crushed tomatoes

4 grams (1 teaspoon) dry Italian seasoning mix, or ¼ teaspoon each of dried oregano, basil, rosemary, and thyme

10 grams (2 teaspoons) fine sea salt

15 grams (1 clove) garlic, minced

20 grams (4 tablespoons) grated Parmesan

Olive oil

1. Preheat the Baking Steel in your oven (page 19).

2. Generously coat a 12-inch cake pan with straight sides with olive oil and place the dough ball in the pan. Using your fingers, stretch the dough to the edges and about three-quarters of the way up the sides of the pan. Let the dough rest 15 minutes, then stretch again. Be patient; it will shrink back.

3. Cover the entire surface of the dough with the mozzarella slices (you don't have to leave room for the crust), and scatter the shredded fontina on top of that.

4. Open your can of tomatoes and add the Italian seasoning mix, salt, and garlic right into the can (no need to dirty another bowl!). Give a quick stir to combine, then pour the sauce over the pizza dough.

5. Use a pizza peel or oven mitts to launch the pan on top of your Baking Steel. Bake for 25 to 30 minutes or until the edges of the crust are browned and crispy.

6. Carefully remove from the oven, sprinkle the grated Parmesan on top, drizzle with olive oil, and let cool for about 15 minutes on top of a wire rack before serving in pie-style wedges.

ONION RING PIZZA

You might think that onion rings and pizza are an unlikely pairing. But if you love both of these things, then I urge you to make this pizza immediately. It's a simple pie, a classic Margherita topped with perfectly crispy, Baking Steel–cooked onion rings coated in seasoned flour and panko-chili bread crumbs. A combination of shredded and torn mozzarella adds visual appeal, and the crispy-crunchy onions offer a pungent flavor and titillating texture.

MAKES ONE 12-INCH PIZZA

1 ball Seventy-Two-Hour Pizza Dough or your favorite pizza dough

Flour for dusting

¼ cup tomato sauce

110 grams (4 ounces) fresh mozzarella

10 to 12 onion rings (recipe follows)

4 or 5 basil leaves

Olive oil

1. Preheat the Baking Steel in your oven (page 19).

2. Stretch your dough into a 12-inch circle (oblong or oval is also fine). Lightly flour your peel and place the dough on top.

3. Set the oven to Broil.

4. Evenly distribute the tomato sauce across the top of the pizza, leaving about 1 inch around the perimeter for the crust.

5. Tear about two-thirds of the mozzarella into pieces and place evenly across the sauced surface. Less is more; it will ooze in the oven's heat. Shred the remaining mozzarella and reserve.

6. Use a generously floured pizza peel to launch your pizza onto the Baking Steel and bake under the broiler for 2 minutes.

7. After 2 minutes, open the oven and use your pizza peel to give the pizza a 180-degree turn. Place onion rings on top and scatter the shredded mozzarella around the rings. Turn off the broiler, set the oven to its highest temperature, and continue cooking for another 1 to 2 minutes or until the cheese has attained the desired brownness.

8. Use your pizza peel to remove the pie from the oven. Garnish with basil leaves and a drizzle of olive oil, then slice and serve.

1 large sweet onion

To coat

1 cup buttermilk

Seasoned flour

120 grams (1 cup) all-purpose flour

Fine sea salt and pepper

15 grams (1 teaspoon) chili powder

Egg wash

3 whole eggs, lightly beaten

Bread crumbs

120 grams (1 cup) panko bread crumbs

Fine sea salt and pepper

15 grams (1 teaspoon) chili powder

Olive oil

1. Preheat the Baking Steel in your oven (page 19).

2. Line a baking sheet with parchment paper.

3. Set up your work space with four medium, shallow bowls. Pour the buttermilk into the first. Sift the seasoned-flour ingredients into a second. Place the lightly beaten eggs in the third. Stir together the bread-crumb ingredients in the fourth.

4. Slice the onion into rings about ½ inch thick.

5. Dip the rings, one at a time, into each of the four bowls. Start by soaking the ring in the buttermilk, then dip it in the flour mixture, then in the egg wash, and finally dip it into the bread crumbs.

6. Place the coated rings on your baking sheet, and use a pizza peel or oven mitts to launch the sheet on top of your Baking Steel. Bake, without flipping, for 6 minutes or until toasted (since you'll be cooking them on the pizza again, leave them a little room to continue browning). Set aside.

SPICY COCONUT SHRIMP
AND LEEK PIZZA

Seafood on pizza isn't a new phenomenon. In Connecticut, clam pizza has been a regional specialty for years. In the 1980s, fancy restaurants jumped on the bandwagon, offering shrimp-and-seafood-topped pies that raised pizza from kid-party food to haute cuisine.

When I was slinging pizza at Figs in the nineties and early aughts, spicy shrimp pizza was one of our most popular offerings. Something about the spice and the juicy texture of shrimp on pizza proved irresistible. Well, the combo still works, so I'm going to leak this secret to you with a few little twists of my own. I've created a spicy coconut coating for the shrimp and combined it with leeks for a flavor that will blow you away.

MAKES ONE 12-INCH PIZZA

1 ball Thin-Crust Pizza Dough (page 42)

Flour for dusting

¼ cup No-Cook Tomato Sauce (page 48)

15 grams (1 tablespoon) crushed red pepper flakes, plus additional for seasoning the tomato sauce

5 to 9 small to medium shrimp, peeled and deveined

100 grams (1 medium) leek, thinly sliced, outer green leaves discarded

25 to 40 grams (about ¼ cup) bread crumbs

15 grams (1 tablespoon) shredded unsweetened coconut

Olive oil

1. Preheat the Baking Steel in your oven (page 19).

2. On a lightly floured work surface, shape the dough by hand into a circle roughly 5 inches in diameter. Then, using a rolling pin, roll it horizontally and vertically to work it into a circle about ⅛ inch thick and 11 to 12 inches across. Knock out any additional air bubbles by hand. Lift your dough onto a lightly floured pizza peel.

3. Season your tomato sauce with red pepper flakes to taste. Evenly distribute the tomato sauce across the top of the pizza, leaving about 1 inch around the perimeter for the crust.

4. Evenly distribute the shrimp and leek slices across the top. Scatter the surface with bread crumbs.

5. Use a generously floured pizza peel to launch your pizza onto the Baking Steel and bake under the broiler for 2 minutes.

6. After 2 minutes, open the oven and use your pizza peel to give the pizza a 180-degree turn. While the oven door is open, carefully scatter the coconut on top. Turn off the broiler, set the oven to its highest temperature, and continue cooking for another 1 to 2 minutes, or until the pizza has attained the desired brownness.

7. Use your pizza peel to remove the pie from the oven. Top with olive oil and the remaining crushed red pepper flakes. Slice and serve.

KALE PIZZA

You know how people who have "found" kale get obnoxious and feel the need to tell the world all about it? I'm one of those people. I'm crazy about kale chips; I adore kale salad; I crave kale smoothies. It's a hardy and hearty vegetable that packs a lot of nutrients with minimal calories. It's also a great counterbalance for my other passion, pizza.

There's only one issue: I'm all about using the broiler to attain a perfectly crisp browned topping and crust, but kale has a tendency to burn. The solution came by way of my friend Kenji López-Alt, who suggested I toss the kale onto the pizza after it had started to cook. That way, the kale is crisp but not burned when the rest of the pie is done.

Be sure to have your ingredients ready before you begin this recipe because topping the pizza with the kale requires you to work swiftly. But you'll be rewarded with a simple, semi-healthy pie that will quickly become a favorite.

MAKES ONE 12-INCH PIZZA

30 grams (1 ounce, or 1 cup loosely packed) fresh kale (we love lacinato, or dinosaur, kale), stemmed, torn into pieces

1 tablespoon olive oil

Fine sea salt and pepper

Crushed red pepper flakes

1 ball Seventy-Two-Hour Pizza Dough or your favorite pizza dough

Flour for dusting

85 to 90 grams (3 ounces) Gruyère, shredded

50 to 75 grams (2 to 3 ounces) fresh mozzarella, torn

25 grams (2 cloves) garlic, thinly sliced

1. Preheat the Baking Steel in your oven (page 19).

2. While the oven preheats, in a large bowl, toss your kale with olive oil to coat, and add salt and pepper and red pepper flakes to taste. Set aside.

3. Stretch your dough into a 12-inch circle (oblong or oval is also fine). Lightly flour your peel and place the dough on top.

4. Set the oven to Broil.

5. Evenly distribute the Gruyère, mozzarella, and garlic on top of the dough, leaving about 1 inch around the perimeter for the crust.

6. Use a generously floured pizza peel to launch your pizza onto the Baking Steel and bake under the broiler for 2 minutes.

7. After 2 minutes, open the oven and use your pizza peel to give the pizza a 180-degree turn. While the oven door is open, distribute the kale evenly over the surface of the pie. Turn off the broiler, set the oven to its highest temperature, and continue cooking for another 1 to 2 minutes or until the kale reaches the desired color. I love a little char, which will crisp up that kale nicely.

8. Use your pizza peel to remove the pie from the oven. Slice and serve.

CHEESEBURGER PIZZA

Pizza and burgers together at long and delicious last. This pizza packs a one-two punch of party-food flavor by combining cheeseburger fixings on a perfectly cooked pizza.

The burger part is inspired by a fast-food burger but it isn't the Frankenfood you'd get at a chain. It's made with quality ingredients and will remind you what a great roadside burger should taste like. Kids like it, teenagers adore it, and adults love it.

MAKES ONE 12-INCH PIZZA

1 ball Seventy-Two-Hour Pizza Dough or your favorite pizza dough

Flour for dusting

¼ cup tomato sauce

125 grams (4 ounces) ground beef (we prefer 85 percent lean)

50 grams (2 ounces) of your favorite cheese blend, shredded (we use half fontina, half Muenster)

25 grams (about 2 tablespoons) onion, diced

75 grams (1 medium) dill pickle, diced

25 grams (1 ounce) iceberg lettuce, chiffonaded (page 67)

1 tablespoon Special Sauce (recipe follows)

1. Preheat the Baking Steel in your oven (page 19).

2. Stretch your dough into a 12-inch circle (oblong or oval is also fine). Lightly flour your peel and place the dough on top.

3. Set the oven to Broil.

4. Evenly distribute the tomato sauce across the top of the pizza, leaving about 1 inch around the perimeter for the crust.

5. Using clean hands, form the ground beef into mini-patties and distribute the patties evenly across the top so that every pizza slice will have a little burger. Scatter the shredded cheese across that, and then the onion and pickle.

6. Use a generously floured pizza peel to launch your pizza onto the Baking Steel and bake under the broiler for 2 minutes.

7. After 2 minutes, open the oven and use your pizza peel to give the pizza a 180-degree turn. Turn off the broiler, set the oven to its highest temperature, and continue cooking for another 1 to 2 minutes or until the cheese has attained the desired brownness.

8. Use your pizza peel to remove the pie from the oven. Scatter the lettuce on top. Drizzle with the Special Sauce. Slice and serve.

SPECIAL SAUCE

To make the Special Sauce, combine equal parts ketchup, mayonnaise, and yellow mustard. While you need only about a tablespoon to finish this pie, it's pretty addictive, so it can't hurt to have a little extra on hand.

STROMBOLI

I met Jenn Louis, a *Food and Wine* magazine's Best New Chef of 2012, in a most modern way: Instagram. She had a trade in mind: she'd be willing to share some of her outstanding recipes if I would send her a Baking Steel to test-drive. I thought about that for all of two seconds and then I asked, "Where do I send it?"

A few days later, Chef Louis posted a picture on Instagram of a stromboli she'd made on her Baking Steel for a staff lunch. In short order, I made one myself and served it for lunch to the contractors building our Baking Steel test kitchen. We all agreed: this stromboli recipe is killer.

If you live in or near Portland, Oregon, or if you go there for a visit, I insist that you stop by Chef Louis's Lincoln Restaurant or the Sunshine Tavern, and tell her I sent you. But in the meantime, let me introduce you via this stromboli recipe to the culinary genius that is Jenn Louis. It won't disappoint!

SERVES 8 TO 10

1 ball Seventy-Two-Hour Pizza Dough or your favorite pizza dough

25 grams (1 tablespoon) brown mustard

Fine sea salt and pepper

50 grams (3 thin slices) provolone

50 grams (3 thin slices) soppressata

25 grams (¼ onion) red onion, sliced very thin

15 grams (8 thin slices) jalapeño

50 grams (4 thin slices) uncured ham (I suggest Niman Ranch ham)

Olive oil

Flour for dusting

Tomato sauce (for serving)

1. Preheat the Baking Steel in your oven (page 19).

2. Stretch the dough into a long, skinny oval approximately 12 by 6 inches. Place the dough on top of a sheet of parchment paper (it doesn't need to be floured).

3. Spread brown mustard all over the dough, leaving a ¼-inch border around the edges.

4. Sprinkle all over with salt and pepper to taste. Top with the next 5 ingredients, then roll up, jelly-roll-style, and pinch off the ends to form a seal. Brush the top with olive oil.

5. Place the sheet of parchment paper with the stromboli on top of a well-floured pizza peel, and use the peel to launch it onto the Baking Steel. Bake for 12 to 14 minutes, using the pizza peel to rotate every few minutes, until the stromboli is golden brown with some darker, toasty-looking spots on top.

6. Shove your pizza peel under the parchment to remove the stromboli from the oven. Let it cool for a few minutes, then slice into thick diagonals and serve with tomato sauce.

CRISPY CALZONE

This calzone is a marvel. You assemble a simple Margherita pizza, then, with one action—folding the dough over the fillings—you turn it into something entirely different, a sort of supersize pizza roll with a gooey, cheesy, saucy filling that can't be beat.

Here, the Baking Steel makes an already excellent food even better. Consider the gooey cheese, the sweet-tart tomato sauce, and the fresh basil. Now imagine it wrapped in crispy-on-the-edges dough, the kind that you can attain only with the searing power of steel. Suddenly, this pizza revolution becomes revolutionary all over again.

SERVES 2

1 ball Seventy-Two-Hour Pizza Dough or your favorite pizza dough

⅓ cup No-Cook Tomato Sauce (page 48)

150 grams (5 ounces) fresh mozzarella, torn

15 grams (5 to 8 medium leaves) fresh basil

Olive oil

1. Preheat the Baking Steel in your oven (page 19).

2. Stretch your dough into a 12-inch circle (oblong or oval is also fine). Place on top of a sheet of parchment paper (it doesn't need to be floured).

3. Distribute the sauce in a semicircle over half of the dough, leaving a ¼-inch border around the edges. Place the mozzarella on top of the sauce and the basil leaves on top of that. Fold the uncovered portion of the dough over the toppings and press with your fingers to crimp the edges together and form a seal. Be sure there are no holes in the seal so that none of your tasty fillings ooze out. Brush the top of the calzone with olive oil.

4. Place the calzone (still on the parchment) on top of a lightly floured pizza peel and launch it onto the Baking Steel.

5. Bake for 5 to 6 minutes or until crispy on top.

6. Shove your pizza peel under the parchment to remove the calzone from the oven. Let cool for a few minutes, then slice and serve.

VERY BERRY DESSERT PIZZA

Dessert pizza is typically the stuff of annoying chain restaurants, so a lot of foodies turn their noses up at the idea (and with good reason). But I promise you, this dessert pizza is legit, and it is worth your time.

The secret to success in this recipe is simplicity. We're not going into chocolate-drizzled or candy-coated territory here. Instead, a round of homemade dough is topped with berries and fresh ricotta, then finished with lemon juice and a dusting of confectioners' sugar. It's simple, and yet when the sweet, tart, and creamy flavors come together in your mouth, it's perfect.

MAKES ONE 12-INCH PIZZA

1 ball Seventy-Two-Hour Pizza Dough or your favorite pizza dough

Flour for dusting

85 to 100 grams (3 ounces, or roughly ½ cup loosely packed) fresh blueberries

85 to 100 grams (3 ounces, or roughly ½ cup loosely packed) fresh raspberries

25 grams (1 tablespoon) granulated sugar

150 grams (3 ounces) fresh ricotta

1 tablespoon fresh lemon juice

25 grams (1 ounce) confectioners' sugar

½ lemon

1. Preheat the Baking Steel in your oven (page 19).

2. Stretch your dough into a 12-inch circle (oblong or oval is also fine). Lightly flour your peel and place the dough on top. Set the oven to Broil.

3. In a large bowl, toss all the berries together with the granulated sugar. Carefully place berry mixture on top of your pizza, leaving 1 inch around the perimeter for the crust.

4. In a medium bowl, using a spoon or spatula, mix the ricotta with the lemon juice and confectioners' sugar, then dollop on the pizza.

5. Use a generously floured pizza peel to launch your pizza onto the Baking Steel and bake under the broiler for 2 minutes.

6. After 2 minutes, open the oven and use your pizza peel to give the pizza a 180-degree turn. Turn off the broiler, set the oven to its highest temperature, and continue cooking for another 1 to 2 minutes or until it has attained the desired brownness.

7. Use your pizza peel to remove the pie from the oven. Using a vegetable peeler, remove strips of zest from the lemon. Cut the strips into matchsticks for garnish. Slice the pie and serve.

What to Do with Excess Pizza Dough?

Excess pizza dough. When you teach as many pizza classes and develop as many recipes as I do, it can be a very real problem. After several days, the dough's gluten deteriorates a bit, making for crust that lacks the perfect "chew." Happily, there are delicious solutions; once the dough is past its prime for making pies, it's perfect for making grissini, ciabatta bread, or a truly spectacular tomato focaccia. Should you find yourself with a surplus of dough, these three recipes put it to delectable use.

While these recipes call for our Seventy-Two-Hour Pizza Dough, they will work equally well with our Whole-Wheat Pizza Dough, Sourdough Pizza Dough, or I Want Pizza Tonight Dough, should you find yourself with extra.

GRISSINI

Grissini are long, thin, artisanal bread sticks. They make the best of the complexity of flavors that have developed in the dough, and since they are baked until quite crispy, the lack of chewiness isn't important.

They're incredibly easy to make: simply roll 'em and cut 'em and bake 'em on your Baking Steel; within minutes, you'll have an addictive snack. If you happen to find yourself with a leftover portion of dough that is advancing in age, give it new life with this recipe.

MAKES ABOUT TWENTY 10-INCH-LONG BREAD STICKS

Handful of semolina flour

Handful of bread flour

1 ball Seventy-Two-Hour Pizza Dough or your favorite pizza dough

1. Position a rack in the middle of your oven and place the Baking Steel on top. Preheat oven to 400°F for 45 to 60 minutes.

2. Lightly dust a piece of parchment with a little bit of each of the semolina and bread flours, then place the dough on top. Using both hands, gently stretch the dough in opposite directions until it is about 10 inches long, then, working in the other direction, stretch the top and bottom halves of the dough until it is about 8 inches wide, forming a rectangular shape.

3. Lightly coat the dough on top with a bit more of both flours. Using a bench scraper or a sharp knife, cut the dough into ¼-inch-wide strips lengthwise. Each one should be about 10 inches long.

4. Arrange the dough strips on the parchment paper so that none of them are sticking together (to prevent conjoined bread sticks).

5. Place the parchment with the dough strips on top of a pizza peel, and use it to launch the parchment onto the Baking Steel.

6. Bake for 10 minutes, then open the oven and use the pizza peel to rotate the parchment. Bake for 5 more minutes or until browned to your liking.

7. Use your pizza peel to remove the parchment with the grissini from the oven. Transfer to a wire rack to cool before serving.

8. Store in a paper bag for 3 days or wrap in plastic wrap and freeze for up to a month.

NOTE Dough that is five to fifteen days old is ideal for making grissini; anything fresher should be used for pizza.

CIABATTA BREAD

If bread sticks aren't the mac to your cheese, then I've got another recipe that will make great use of your leftover pizza dough: a loaf of ciabatta bread.

Slightly aged pizza dough, between five and fifteen days old, is full of flavor. Unfortunately, it's no longer ideal for making pizza, because the dough has lost its springiness and tight "crumb." However, the more open crumb structure works perfectly for a loaf of airy, tender ciabatta. Served along with olive oil or used to make overstuffed Italian sandwiches, this bread is a fantastic addition to your baking repertoire.

MAKES 1 LOAF

Handful of semolina flour

Handful of bread flour

1 ball Seventy-Two-Hour Pizza Dough or your favorite pizza dough

1. Position a rack in the middle of your oven and place the Baking Steel on top. Preheat oven to 450°F for 45 to 60 minutes.

2. Lightly dust a piece of parchment paper with a little bit of each of the semolina and bread flours, and place the dough on top. Using both hands, stretch or pull the dough in opposite directions, until it is about 8 inches long. Working in the other direction, stretch the dough until it is about 4 inches wide and rectangular in shape.

3. Lightly dust the top of the dough with a bit more of both flours. Let the dough rest on a baking sheet, uncovered, for 15 to 30 minutes before baking.

4. Place the parchment with the dough on a pizza peel, and use it to launch the dough onto the Baking Steel.

5. Bake for 10 minutes, then open the oven, insert the pizza peel under the parchment paper, and rotate the bread. Bake for 5 to 10 minutes longer or until golden on top.

6. Use your pizza peel to remove the ciabatta from the oven. Transfer to a wire rack to cool before serving.

7. Store in a paper bag for up to 3 days or freeze for up to a month.

THE ULTIMATE TOMATO FOCACCIA

If you really want to impress your guests, throw together a recipe that is like bread and pizza had a baby together. A beautiful, party-friendly, delicious baby.

   This is an ideal recipe for late summer, when you have a wealth of fresh, ripe, juicy tomatoes. You can't eat BLTs every day, and you don't want to waste tomatoes' juicy freshness by reducing them all to sauce. This focaccia lets you use a great quantity of tomatoes without adding much else. Salt, pepper, garlic, and olive oil and your tomatoes will be styling on their carbohydrate bed. In this focaccia recipe, the oiled pan and Baking Steel work some serious magic. The oil infuses the dough as it cooks, yielding an almost caramelized texture on the crispy bottom.

MAKES 1 HALF-SHEET TRAY (ABOUT 24 SERVINGS)

¾ cup olive oil

1 recipe Seventy-Two-Hour Pizza Dough

Salt and pepper

700 grams (1½ pounds) garden tomatoes, sliced or wedged

20 grams (about 2 cloves) garlic, sliced paper thin

1. Position a rack in the lower part of your oven and place the Baking Steel on top. Preheat oven to 500°F for 45 to 60 minutes.

2. Pour ¼ cup of the oil on the bottom of a rimmed half-sheet tray. Yup, it's a lot! Place the dough ball on top and roll it gently around in the oil to lightly coat. Cover with plastic wrap (the oil will discourage sticking) and let rest for 1 hour. It will slightly puff up during this time.

3. After dough has rested, press and stretch it to fill the entire half-sheet tray. While you stretch, press down on the dough with your fingers to make some nice-looking divots throughout. Season with salt and pepper to taste.

4. In a large bowl, toss the tomatoes with the remaining olive oil, salt and pepper to taste, and garlic. Distribute the tomatoes all over the top of the dough, pressing them in to make sure that they fuse with the dough during baking.

5. Use a pizza peel or oven mitts to launch the sheet tray on top of the hot Baking Steel and bake for 8 minutes. Open the oven door and use your peel or mitts to rotate the tray. Bake for 7 to 10 minutes more or until the crust has reached the desired doneness. Remove and let cool on a wire rack. Slice into 24 slabs to serve.

3

BREAD

3

BREAD BASICS

Homemade bread is truly one of life's greatest pleasures, from the aroma of activated yeast to the sensation of the dough under your hands to the inimitable pleasure of eating a slice hot from the oven. Bread puts the *art* in *culinary arts* and blends it with a little science and plenty of energy and creativity.

But attaining high-quality bread at home can prove challenging. Home ovens don't hold a candle to the big, hot ovens at commercial bakeries, which use high, evenly distributed heat to yield light and tender loaves. In recent years, an awareness of and interest in making artisan bread have upped the game for home bakers, but that perfectly baked crust has remained elusive. Not anymore. When you use the Baking Steel, your oven is transformed into a heat-distribution powerhouse, mimicking the way a superhot commercial oven can crisp the crust of a loaf of bread without drying out the inside. This means that you can create bakery-caliber bread using your home oven or, in some cases, your stovetop.

Fermenting, Kneading, Punching, Resting, Shaping, and Proofing

Some bread recipes read like a mash-up of spa treatments and a boxer's training regimen: Punch! Knead! Rest! Shape!

Funny as they sound, these are some of the most important steps in making bread, so let's take a minute to break down the meaning of these key terms.

BULK FERMENTATION
This is when you cover the bowl of dough and let it rise, usually fairly early in the recipe. It refers to letting dough ferment as one bulk unit before you move forward with shaping or dividing the dough (if you're making rolls or multiple loaves, for instance). This is when the yeast does most of its work, imparting flavor and structure as carbon dioxide inflates the gluten network. A bulk fermentation period can range from an hour to several hours, and it will depend on the heat of your kitchen. Often, you can judge whether a dough has fermented enough by visual cues.

KNEADING
Why do we knead bread? The short answer is to develop gluten. Flour contains two proteins, gliadin and glutenin, which together form the protein network gluten. When you mix the ingredients of a dough, the network of gluten is loose and disorganized, like your junk drawer. As you work the dough, you organize those gluten strands into a neat matrix, which gives the bread its structure and form and creates space for the dough to rise.

PUNCHING

In spite of the violent-sounding name, this is not supposed to be a knockout punch delivered to your dough. By gently deflating the bubbles of gas formed by the yeast during the bread's first rise, you give the bread a finer texture and help prevent the formation of overly large air bubbles, which can pop during baking and weaken the structure.

To properly punch your dough, press your fist down into it, confidently but smoothly. Then gather the edges around the indent left behind by your fist and wrap them into the center (sort of like you would when making dough balls). Gently remove the dough from the bowl and give it a pat; if it feels very bubbly or airy, you can give it a quick knead or two to knock out any straggling air bubbles.

RESTING

If you have time, let the dough rest ten to fifteen minutes after you punch it down and before you shape it. Cover your dough with an inverted bowl and let it sit on a lightly floured counter. Some doughs are quite elastic and will pull back at first when rolled out. This brief rest will relax the gluten and make the dough easier to roll out and shape.

SHAPING YOUR BREAD DOUGH

Shaping your bread dough refers to forming the bread into the shape you'd like to bake, whether that's braided strands, rolls, or a long cylinder. While this will vary from recipe to recipe, here are some basic tips that might help.

- When dividing dough, use a kitchen scale to make sure each portion weighs the same amount.

- Pinch the seams: Pinch the ends together and smooth out or tuck under the edges of the loaf (so that the seam is facing the counter). This helps keep the bread from spreading out in ways you don't want. You can also use cold water to help seal edges.

PROOFING

Also called *proving*, proofing refers to the final rising period of your dough. This is specifically after the dough has been shaped but before it bakes. It allows the dough—sometimes covered, sometimes uncovered—to puff up slightly and even out so that it doesn't rise into odd angles when put in the oven.

BREAD RECIPES

ENGLISH MUFFINS

I grew up devouring English muffins; I'm not ashamed to confess that at a certain time in my life, I could eat an entire package over the weekend. But as my palate became more refined, I started to find the commercial varieties floppy, flavorless, and generally uninviting. Not the type of stuff I wanted my kids eating. So I went to work developing my own English muffin recipe.

English muffin dough, unlike some other bread doughs, isn't improved by heavy kneading. This minimal handling discourages strong gluten strands from forming, which means a more open structure—and in English muffins, that adds up to nooks and crannies.

The dough, coated in semolina and cooked briefly on the Baking Steel with clarified butter (which has a higher smoke point than regular butter), attains the perfect texture, with a crispy exterior and craggy interior just begging to be filled. This is what store-bought English muffins want to be when they grow up. I make a batch almost every week, and my sons think they are amazing.

MAKES 12 MUFFINS

550 grams (4½ cups) all-purpose flour, plus more for dusting

20 grams (4 teaspoons) fine sea salt

20 grams (4 teaspoons) sugar

1 gram (¼ teaspoon) active dry yeast

1½ tablespoons unsalted butter, melted and slightly cooled

1½ cups water, warm (about 105°F)

165 grams (½ cup) semolina flour

1 cup clarified butter
(see recipe note, page 123)

1. In a large bowl, whisk together the flour, salt, sugar, and yeast.

2. In a separate small bowl, combine the melted butter and warm water. Slowly pour the wet ingredients into the dry ingredients, and mix with a wooden spoon to combine.

3. Lightly flour a work surface, turn the mixture out onto it, and knead by hand for 4 to 5 minutes, until it forms a smooth dough. Let rest for 15 minutes.

4. Meanwhile, lightly coat a baking sheet with semolina flour. Set aside.

5. Divide the dough into 12 equal portions (about 85 grams each).

CONT.

6. Using floured hands, place your palm on a portion of dough and rotate it in a circular motion while pressing down. This will create a ball with no seams. If the dough gets sticky, coat your hand with a little bit more flour. Coat the ball with semolina flour, then place it on the semolina-coated sheet tray. Repeat with the remaining portions of dough.

7. Cover the tray with plastic wrap and let the dough proof for at least 2 to 3 hours. The dough balls will just about double in size. At this point, you can let the dough proof at room temperature for up to 24 hours; if you need more time, you can place the dough in the refrigerator for up to 3 days.

8. Position your Baking Steel Griddle on the stovetop. Preheat on medium heat for 10 to 15 minutes. You're looking for a surface temperature of 275 to 300°F, or until droplets of water sizzle on the surface.

9. Brush or pour some of the clarified butter over the surface of your Baking Steel Griddle. Be generous; you want to coat the entire surface as completely as you can without the butter sloshing over. The butter should begin to lightly bubble as soon as you apply it to the surface.

10. Place the dough balls on the Baking Steel Griddle, a few at a time, and cook for 4 minutes. Once golden on the bottom, flip, adding more clarified butter as needed to allow the dough to swim slightly in butter. After you flip, gently press down on the dough with your spatula to flatten into the signature English muffin shape.

11. Once the second side is golden, remove and transfer to a wire rack to cool.

NOTE This recipe calls for clarified butter, which is butter from which the milk solids have been removed, leaving pure butterfat. No, this isn't just to be fancy. Removing those milk solids gives the butter a higher smoke point, which in this recipe helps ensure that you don't end up with blackened English muffins. If you don't have clarified butter, you can substitute canola or even olive oil.

EXTRA CREDIT **How should you split an English muffin?** Many a recipe claims that one should use a fork. Hogwash! The best way to slice an English muffin is to take a serrated knife and carefully slice around the perimeter, then peel the muffin open with your hands, very carefully and patiently. Voilà! Nooks and crannies revealed.

BAGELS

Many people love bagels, but few know how to make them at home. This is truly tragic, because there is nothing like a fresh-boiled-then-baked bagel. If you've ever been the first customer on line in a New York City bagel shop, you might have had a taste of this perfection, but that experience won't give you the inimitable sense of pride that comes from making your own.

Once the dough has been boiled, finishing up your bagels on the Baking Steel allows for the perfect New York bagel texture: slightly crispy-chewy on the outside, soft and tender on the inside. The recipe starts a day before you actually get to eat the bagels; fermenting the dough overnight gives you a head start on flavor and adds a yeasty aroma that differentiates these bagels from rounds of white bread. Boiling, then baking the bagels gives them an assertive but not overpowering density. Your cream cheese will be honored to grace them.

MAKES 8 LARGE BAGELS

500 grams (3¾ cups) bread flour

12 grams (1½ tablespoons) sugar

1 gram (¼ teaspoon) active dry yeast

16 grams (1 tablespoon) fine sea salt

1 cup water, warm (about 105°F)

DAY 1

1. In a large bowl, whisk together the flour, sugar, yeast, and salt.

2. Make a well in the center of the dry ingredients and pour in the water. Mix with a wooden spoon just to combine, then knead the dough by hand on a lightly floured countertop or cutting board for about 5 minutes, until it is smooth and elastic.

3. Put the dough in a bowl and cover with a clean, damp kitchen towel or plastic wrap. Allow to rise at room temperature for 24 hours or until the dough has just about doubled in size.

DAY 2

4. Preheat your oven to 425°F for 45 to 60 minutes with your Baking Steel inside.

5. Punch the dough down, and let it rest for another 10 minutes.

6. Divide the dough into 8 equal portions. Form dough into balls.

7. Coat a finger in flour and poke a hole in the center of each dough ball, then gently stretch the hole with your fingers to form a traditional bagel shape.

8. After shaping the dough rounds and placing them on a piece of parchment paper, cover with a damp kitchen towel and allow them to rest for 10 minutes.

9. Bring a large pot of water to a boil. Use a slotted spoon or skimmer to lower the bagels into the water. Boil for about 1 minute; the bagels will rise in the water and may bob on top. Using a slotted spoon, remove the bagels, tap them to remove excess water, and transfer to a lightly oiled piece of parchment paper. If you'd like to add seeds or toppings to your bagels, now is the time; right after boiling is when they will be stickiest and best able to hold on to them.

10. Either place your parchment on a sheet tray and place that on your Baking Steel or use a pizza peel to launch the parchment sheet directly onto your Baking Steel.

11. Bake for 14 to 16 minutes—rotating halfway through baking—or until golden brown. Remove and transfer to a wire rack.

12. Cool completely and make sure you have some soft cream cheese around. Store in an airtight container for 3 to 5 days or freeze for up to a month.

EXTRA CREDIT For a bagel to truly be a bagel, it must be boiled before it is baked. Why? A brief boiling (typically less than a minute) forms a gel-like surface on the outside of the bagel (just look at one after boiling; it's gummy in texture). Once the dough is baked, this gel sets into the bagel's signature chewy, dense texture.

Some types of bagels, especially commercially produced varieties, are steamed instead of boiled to streamline the process. The texture is comparable although not quite the same as a boiled bagel. But if the manufacturer forgoes the boiling process entirely? It might be a tasty ring of bread, but that's all it is. It's not a bagel.

DEMI-BAGUETTES

A baguette is not merely a long, thin loaf of white bread. The flavor secret lies in the bread starter—in this case, a *poolish*, which is made with equal parts water and flour, by weight. It imparts a complex, well-rounded flavor to the baguette or, as here, the demi-baguettes (the cute French term for mini-baguettes). As you do with a sourdough starter, be sure to start your *poolish* two days before you want your bread!

The ideal baguette is crusty on the outside, pillowy and slightly chewy on the inside. The Baking Steel helps you attain this in two ways. First, when the bread hits the heat of the steel, it instantly sets on the bottom, which causes the loaf to puff and attain a perfect cylindrical shape. Second, the equal heat dispersion of the Baking Steel helps the bread bake evenly, so the coloring is perfect on the exterior and the interior is not overcooked. A quick spray of water on the dough just before you close the oven door helps the bread set with a crust that is firm but won't tear the roof of your mouth when you take a bite.

MAKES THREE 14- TO 16-INCH BAGUETTES

Poolish

100 grams (¾ cup) all-purpose flour

0.25 gram (pinch) instant yeast

½ cup water, at room temperature

Baguettes

150 grams (1 cup) bread flour

150 grams (1¼ cups) all-purpose flour

1 gram (¼ teaspoon) instant yeast

8 grams (about 1½ teaspoons) fine sea salt

¾ cup water, warm (about 105°F)

Spray bottle with water

1. To make the *poolish,* combine the flour and yeast in a large bowl. With a wooden spoon, gradually mix in the water. Let it sit at room temperature for two days in an airtight container.

2. To make the dough, combine the flours, yeast, and salt in the bowl of a mixer fitted with the dough-hook attachment. Add the *poolish* mixture and about half the water and mix on low for 3 minutes, gradually adding the rest of the water as you mix.

3. Scrape down the bowl with a rubber spatula and continue to mix on low for 6 to 8 minutes. The dough should come together in a smooth ball and spring back slightly when indented with a finger.

4. Place the dough in a lightly oiled bowl and cover with a clean kitchen towel or plastic wrap. Allow to rest for 1 hour.

5. After an hour, turn the dough out onto a floured work surface. Punch the dough down and flatten it into a rectangle with your hands. Fold it horizontally into thirds—the way you would a business letter—and press with the palm of your hand to seal. Allow the dough to rest on the countertop, covered with a clean, damp kitchen towel, for an hour and then repeat the fold, resting after, for a total of 4 folds.

6. Preheat the oven for 45 to 60 minutes at 460°F with the Baking Steel inside (so that I don't forget, I often do this right after the second folding).

7. Directly after performing the third folding, divide your dough into 3 equal portions (about 245 grams each) and shape each portion into a long, thin roll about 15 inches long. Let rest for 10 minutes.

8. Use a bread *lame* or a razor blade to mark the top of your bread with three diagonal slits, about 4 inches apart.

9. Using a pizza peel, launch each baguette onto the hot Baking Steel. Just before closing the oven door, use the spray bottle to spritz the steel with water to create a burst of steam.

10. Bake for about 18 minutes, using a pizza peel to rotate the loaves halfway through baking. Once the loaves are golden on top, remove from the oven and transfer to a wire rack to cool completely.

11. Store at room temperature in a paper bag for 2 to 3 days or freeze for up to a month.

What Are Pre-Ferments (and Are They Worth It)?

A pre-ferment (such as the *poolish* used above) is a small portion of dough that is made in advance, sometimes several hours or even days ahead. Depending on the ingredients used, it can have a stiff, Play-Doh-like texture or it can be almost liquid.

Waiting for hours or days for a pre-ferment to develop can be annoying, and it does beg the question: Is it worth it? I vote yes. While it might seem like wasted time, your pre-ferment is actually giving you a head start on bread making. Allowing the yeasts to develop imparts a more deeply yeasty, sour note to your bread (like sourdough), which adds a lot of flavor and complexity. This can be the difference between "tastes good for homemade" and truly professional-quality bread.

The *poolish*, favored by most French bakeries, is the most common pre-ferment. It imparts a moist crumb, a tender, not gummy chew, and great all-around flavor.

BUTTERMILK BISCUITS

I love biscuits just as much as I love pizza. I don't say this lightly. There's something so simple and perfect about biscuits: they can act as a vessel for just about anything, savory or sweet, sandwich or dessert. A truly great biscuit, though, should be able to stand on its own. This recipe produces that biscuit.

The ingredient list is short and sweet, and the basic theory behind biscuit dough is the less you handle it, the better. The hot Baking Steel browns the bottom of the buttery dough, making it set and crisp quickly, so you have a satisfying crust but a feathery soft interior. The finished biscuits are sturdy enough that they won't become soggy when topped with gravy, but soft enough that they taste like a dream if you use them for strawberry shortcake. The recipe is already a winner, but making it on the Baking Steel propels it into best-ever territory.

MAKES ABOUT TWELVE 4-INCH BISCUITS

625 grams (5 cups) all-purpose flour

24 grams (2 tablespoons) baking powder

8 grams (2 teaspoons) baking soda

10 grams (2 teaspoons) fine sea salt

24 tablespoons unsalted butter, cold, cut into cubes

1¾ cups buttermilk, plus more for brushing

1. Position the Baking Steel on the middle rack of your oven. Preheat the oven to 400°F for 45 to 60 minutes.

2. In the bowl of a food processor or in a large mixing bowl, combine the flour, baking powder, baking soda, and salt. Pulse in the processor a few times or stir with a whisk to incorporate.

3. Add the cubed butter while slowly pulsing the food processor until the mixture looks like pebbly sand. Do not overmix; it will cream the butter too much

CONT.

and make your biscuits cookie-like. Alternatively, you can combine the ingredients by cutting cubes of butter into the dry ingredients with two forks or a pastry cutter.

4. If using a food processor, transfer the mixture to a large mixing bowl. Create a well in the center of the mixture and pour in the buttermilk. Slowly incorporate the buttermilk into your dry mixture; I find that mixing with my fingers works best.

5. Once the mixture comes together in a shaggy ball, turn the dough onto a lightly floured cutting board or kitchen counter. Roll the dough out to about ¾ inch thick with a rolling pin.

6. Cut the biscuits out with a biscuit cutter, cookie cutter, or knife. I like to use a 4-inch-diameter biscuit cutter; in a pinch, you can use an inverted, wide-mouth drinking glass with a floured rim. Be careful not to wiggle or twist the cutter too much as you make your cutouts; it can prevent the biscuits from rising in flaky layers.

7. Place the biscuits on top of a sheet of parchment paper. Brush the tops of the biscuits lightly with buttermilk.

8. Either put your parchment on a sheet tray and place on your Baking Steel or use a pizza peel to launch the parchment directly onto your steel. Bake for 14 minutes—rotating halfway through baking—or until golden brown on the top and bottom.

9. When the biscuits are done, remove the parchment and transfer the biscuits to a wire rack to cool completely.

10. Store well-wrapped leftovers at room temperature for up to 2 days or freeze for up to 1 month.

PUMPERNICKEL BREAD

Did you know that a rough translation of *pumpernickel* is "devil's fart"? This bread comes from Germany, where the word *pumpern* refers to, well, breaking wind; *nickel* is derived from Nicholas, a name in German folklore that's associated with goblins and other devilish characters. The word alludes to the effects of this dark, rye-enriched bread on the digestive system.

Don't let fear of farting keep you from enjoying this loaf, which is the perfect canvas for a sandwich. It has an amazingly complex flavor owing to coffee, molasses, and cocoa powder, and the Baking Steel ensures that it has a perfect texture, airy on the inside but crisp on the outside.

MAKES ONE 10-INCH LOAF

250 grams (2 cups) bread flour

125 grams (1¼ cups) medium rye flour

15 grams (2 tablespoons) unsweetened cocoa powder

6 grams (1½ teaspoons) sugar

8 grams (1½ teaspoons) fine sea salt

2 grams (½ teaspoon) active dry yeast

¾ cup plus 2 tablespoons brewed coffee, at room temperature

2 tablespoons olive oil

2 tablespoons dark molasses

DAY 1

1. In a large bowl, whisk together the flours, cocoa powder, sugar, salt, and yeast.

2. In a medium bowl, whisk together the coffee, olive oil, and molasses, mixing until incorporated. Add the wet ingredients to the dry and mix using a wooden spoon until totally incorporated.

3. Turn the dough out onto a floured work surface and knead for 5 to 6 minutes by hand (alternatively, 3 to 4 minutes on medium speed in the bowl of a stand mixer fitted with the dough hook). In kneading, you want to remove any dry clumps and form a nice, tight ball. The dough won't be quite as elastic as a dough made entirely with a bread flour or even whole-wheat flour; it's just the nature of rye flour. Go with it. Cover your dough with a damp, clean kitchen towel or plastic wrap and let rise at room temperature for 24 hours.

DAY 2

4. Turn the risen dough mixture onto a floured work surface.

5. With floured hands, shape the dough into a large ball by folding the sides in and pinching them in the center to form a seam. Place the ball, seam-side up, in a

CONT.

floured breadbasket and cover with a damp towel. Let rest for 2 more hours.

6. Position a rack in the middle of your oven and place the Baking Steel on top. Preheat oven to 425°F for 45 to 60 minutes.

7. Turn the dough onto a floured pizza peel, seam-side down. With a bread *lame* or a razor blade, make 2 to 3 slits across the dough, cutting ⅛ inch deep.

8. Use the pizza peel to launch your bread onto the hot Baking Steel.

9. Bake for 20 to 25 minutes, using the peel to rotate the steel halfway through baking. Since this bread is dark in color, detecting doneness can be difficult. I like to knock on the top of it when I think it's about done; if it is, it will have a slightly hollow sound.

10. Remove the bread using a pizza peel and transfer to a wire rack to let cool completely.

11. Store in a paper bag for up to 3 days or freeze for up to 1 month.

EXTRA CREDIT What's a breadbasket? Also known as a *banneton* or *brotform*, a breadbasket is a wicker bowl-shaped basket that contains dough while it rises. It not only discourages the sideways spread of wetter doughs, but imparts a beautiful spiral pattern on top of the dough that contrasts nicely with slash marks and makes your bread look bakery-bought. If you don't happen to own (or don't want to own) a breadbasket, a large (about ten inches in diameter) floured bowl will work just fine.

RYE BREAD

If you think that rye bread is merely a vehicle for pastrami, you've got it wrong. Rye bread is one of the most subtle breads I can think of, and while it's a great sandwich bread, it's just as good alone, lightly toasted and slathered with butter.

A touch of molasses and a mix of caraway seeds, fennel, anise, and dried orange peel give this bread a spicy flavor that works well with the slight astringency of the rye flour.

MAKES ONE 10-INCH LOAF

350 grams (2¾ cups) all-purpose flour

135 grams (1 cup) rye flour

2 grams (½ teaspoon) active dry yeast

16 grams (1 tablespoon) fine sea salt

6 grams (1 teaspoon) each of caraway, fennel, anise, and dried orange peel, mixed together and ground in a spice grinder

1½ cups whole milk

4 tablespoons butter, cut into pieces

¼ cup dark molasses

Special equipment

Breadbasket (optional; see note on page 135)

DAY 1

1. In a large bowl, whisk together the flours, yeast, salt, and spice mixture.

2. In a medium saucepan, combine the milk, butter, and molasses. Cook over medium heat until the butter has just melted and the ingredients are fully combined.

3. Remove from heat; add the milk mixture to the dry mixture and stir with a wooden spoon until completely combined.

4. Turn the dough mixture out onto a floured work surface and knead for 5 to 6 minutes by hand (alternatively, you can mix for 3 to 4 minutes on medium speed in the bowl of a stand mixer fitted with the dough hook). You want to remove any dry clumps and form a nice, tight ball. Place in a lightly oiled bowl, cover with a damp kitchen towel or plastic wrap, and let rise at room temperature for 24 hours.

DAY 2

5. Turn the risen dough mixture out onto a floured work surface.

6. With floured hands, shape the dough into a large ball by folding the sides in and tucking the seam up. Place the ball, seam-side up, in a floured breadbasket or large bowl and cover with a damp kitchen towel. Let rest for 2 more hours.

7. Position a rack in the middle of your oven and place the Baking Steel on top. Preheat oven to 425°F for 45 to 60 minutes.

8. Turn the dough out onto a floured pizza peel, seam-side down. With a bread *lame* or a razor blade, make 2 to 3 slits, ⅛ inch deep, across the top of the dough.

9. Use a lightly floured pizza peel to launch the dough onto the hot Baking Steel.

10. Bake for 20 to 25 minutes, using a peel to rotate the bread halfway through baking. Since this bread is dark in color, detecting doneness can be difficult. I like to knock on the top of it when I think it's about done; if it is, it will have a slightly hollow sound.

11. Remove the bread using a pizza peel and transfer to a wire rack to let cool completely.

12. Store in a paper bag for up to 3 days or freeze for up to 1 month.

COUNTRY BREAD BOULE

This is an extremely easy loaf of bread to make, and baked on the Baking Steel, it has a crusty, inimitable texture that will fill you with pride; you won't believe you were able to attain this crust at home! It's perfect for sandwiches or served warm with olive oil for dipping.

MAKES ONE 10-INCH LOAF

500 grams (3¾ cups) bread flour

16 grams (1 tablespoon) fine sea salt

1 gram (¼ teaspoon) active dry yeast

1¾ cups water, warm (about 105°F)

Special equipment

Breadbasket (optional; see note on page 135)

DAY 1

1. In a large bowl, whisk together the flour, salt, and yeast.

2. Slowly add the water and mix with a wooden spoon to just combine.

3. Turn the dough out onto a floured work surface and knead for 5 to 6 minutes by hand (alternatively, you can mix for 3 to 4 minutes on medium speed in the bowl of a stand mixer fitted with the dough hook). You want to remove any dry clumps and form a nice, tight ball. Place in a lightly oiled bowl, cover with a damp kitchen towel or plastic wrap, and let rise at room temperature for 24 hours.

DAY 2

4. Turn the risen dough mixture out onto a floured work surface.

5. With floured hands, shape the dough into a large ball by folding the sides in. Place the ball, seam-side up, in a floured breadbasket and cover with a damp towel. Let rest for 2 more hours.

6. Halfway through the resting period, position a rack in the middle of your oven and place the Baking Steel on top. Preheat oven to 400°F for 45 to 60 minutes.

7. Turn the dough onto a lightly floured pizza peel, seam-side down. With a bread *lame* or a razor blade, make 2 to 3 slits across the top of the dough, cutting ⅛ inch deep.

8. Use the pizza peel to launch the dough onto your Baking Steel. Bake for 20 to 25 minutes, rotating halfway through that time to ensure even baking. Remove from the oven with a pizza peel, transfer to a wire rack, and let cool completely before serving.

9. Store in a paper bag at room temperature for up to 3 days or freeze up to 1 month.

What's a *Lame* and What Does It Do?

Not to be confused with a teenage dismissal or a disco clothing material, a *lame* (pronounced "lahm" in your Frenchiest accent) is a razorlike tool used to score bread before baking. Scoring your bread does more than just up its visual appeal; it also controls how the dough expands while baking, allowing the bread to release steam and bake evenly.

If you don't have a *lame*, don't sweat it. You can use a razor, a serrated knife, or the blade edge of a pair of kitchen shears to do the job.

Here are a few common cuts that you can use for your loaves.

SLASHES
This one's simple: Make evenly spaced diagonal slashes along the length of your loaf. Traditionally, it's four slashes, and the slashing method is most effective on a long loaf, such as a baguette. This allows for even sideways expansion.

CROSS-HATCHING
For oblong loaves such as boules, slashes don't quite do it; you need a crisscross pattern that allows the loaf to expand upward and outward. To do this, use your *lame* to draw lines vertically and then horizontally across the top of the loaf (or in opposing diagonal directions).

LEAF
This reminds me of how you would draw leaves when you were in elementary school. Start with one long slash along the vertical length of the bread, then draw diagonal lines upward on each side. This allows for upward and outward expansion of the bread.

STARBURST
This cut reminds me of cutting a pizza! Leaving the center untouched, make cuts along the surface of the bread so that there are eight equal wedges. When it bakes up, you'll have a lovely starburst pattern. You can make it extra fancy by using a curved *lame* to make the lines.

WHITE BREAD

White bread has a lot of negative connotations, largely owing to the plastic-wrapped, sugar-filled stuff lining the shelves of grocery stores. But when it's homemade, a basic white bread can truly be one of life's greatest pleasures. Baking this loaf in a covered *pain de mie* pan helps it attain a tender texture and soft crust that will satisfy your sense of nostalgia but give you a flavor leagues above the stuff you find in the store.

Use this bread to bookend your kid's peanut butter and jelly sandwiches, or load a slice up with butter and toss it under the broiler for a few minutes for a thoroughly perfect snack.

MAKES 1 MEDIUM LOAF

520 grams (4¼ cups) all-purpose flour

50 grams (½ cup) potato flour

50 grams (½ cup) dry milk powder

35 grams (3 tablespoons) sugar

16 grams (1 tablespoon) fine sea salt

1½ grams (½ teaspoon) instant yeast

⅔ cup milk

1 cup water, warm (about 105°F)

8 tablespoons unsalted butter, melted

Special equipment

13-inch *pain de mie* pan or loaf pan (see note)

DAY 1

1. In the bowl of a stand mixer fitted with the dough-hook attachment or in a large mixing bowl, mix the flours, milk powder, sugar, salt, and yeast, and whisk to combine.

2. With the mixer running on low, add the milk, water, and melted butter and mix on medium speed for 3 to 4 minutes to form a smooth, soft dough that begins to pull away from the sides of the bowl. (Alternatively, add the milk, water, and melted butter while whisking and then knead 6 to 8 minutes by hand.)

3. Lightly oil or wet your hands to prevent sticking, transfer the dough to an oiled bowl, cover with a damp towel, and let rise for 1 hour.

4. Lightly grease a 13-inch loaf pan.

5. Gently punch down the dough, transfer it to a lightly floured work surface, shape it into a 13-inch-long log, and fit it into the pan, seam-side down. Cover the pan with lightly greased plastic wrap and allow the dough to rise for 24 hours. Once risen, it should reach just below the lip of the pan.

DAY 2

6. Position a rack in the middle of your oven and place the Baking Steel on top. Preheat oven to 350°F for 45 to 60 minutes.

7. Remove the plastic from the dough. Lightly grease the cover of the pan and place it on top.

8. Bake the bread for 35 minutes, rotating halfway through baking. Remove the pan from the oven, carefully remove the lid, and return the bread to the oven to bake for an additional 10 minutes. Then remove the bread from the oven and place the pan on a wire rack to cool.

9. Store well-wrapped leftovers at room temperature for up to 3 days or freeze for up to 1 month.

EXTRA CREDIT **What's a *pain de mie* pan?** A *pain de mie* pan, also called a pullman pan, is a sealed loaf pan. The name *pain de mie* translates to "bread of the crumb," and the almost cakelike texture of bread baked in this pan is certainly unique. The lid keeps a healthy level of humidity contained in the bread, which means that the edges aren't going to toast as rapidly, so the crust will be soft, and the interior of the bread is super-tender. It's similar to the effect that you get if you tent foil over the edges of a pie crust to keep it from crisping too much. If you don't have a *pain de mie* pan, you can use a 13-inch loaf pan and simply cover the top with foil. It may yield a slightly drier loaf, but it will do in a pinch.

BRIOCHE, THREE WAYS

For me, brioche is forever "the butter bread." Bread dough is simply flour, water, and yeast, but brioche dough is bread dough enriched with butter, milk, and eggs. The amount of fat added fills it with flavor and gives it an impossibly tender texture.

The light texture makes the bread highly absorbent, ideal for hamburger and hot-dog buns or gooey, flavorful cinnamon rolls. In these recipes, you'll start with the same basic dough, and from there, you can decide to make a traditional pullman loaf, cinnamon rolls, or fluffy dinner rolls.

MAKES 1 PULLMAN-STYLE LOAF, ABOUT 16 CINNAMON ROLLS, OR 12 DINNER ROLLS

650 grams (5 cups) bread flour

100 grams (½ cup) sugar

3 grams (1 teaspoon) active dry yeast

16 grams (1 tablespoon) fine sea salt

4 large eggs plus 1 yolk

1 cup milk

18 tablespoons unsalted butter, cubed and softened

DAY 1

1. In the bowl of a stand mixer fitted with the dough hook, combine the bread flour, sugar, yeast, and salt on low speed.

2. With the mixer running on low, add the eggs, yolk, and milk. Increase the speed to medium and mix for 4 minutes. Add the butter and continue mixing until totally combined, 4 to 5 minutes more.

3. Turn the dough onto a floured work surface. With floured hands, form the dough into a ball.

4. Place the dough ball in an airtight container and let it sit in the refrigerator for 18 to 24 hours.

DAY 2

5. Turn the risen dough out of the container onto a floured work surface.

6. Punch down the dough and shape as desired.

From here, you can choose your own adventure; there are a variety of different goodies you can make using this one versatile dough. Look deep inside your heart; which carb do you crave? Is it sweet, gooey cinnamon rolls? Or soft, pillowy dinner rolls, perfect for sliders? Or maybe you want a loaf that you can serve in slices or save for French toast. Choose one of the three options that follow and proceed.

CINNAMON ROLLS

1 recipe Brioche dough

For the filling

220 grams (1 cup firmly packed) light brown sugar

5 grams (2 teaspoons) cinnamon

2½ grams (½ teaspoon) fine sea salt

4 tablespoons unsalted butter, melted

To top

375 grams (3 cups) sifted confectioners' sugar

Pinch of fine sea salt

Heavy cream (amount can vary; start with ¼ cup)

Chopped pecans (optional)

1. Divide the dough in half. Roll out each portion to make a large (about 14 by 6 inches) rectangle.

2. In a small bowl, mix together the brown sugar, cinnamon, and salt. Brush each rectangle with the melted butter and sprinkle with this filling. Starting with the long side, roll up each rectangle into a roll.

3. Cut 1 long roll into 8 equal parts. Place 1 part in the center of a greased cake pan or pie plate, and place the remaining parts in a circle around it. Do the same with the second roll. (Alternatively, use a single larger pan.) Cover with plastic wrap and let the rolls proof in the pans at room temperature for about 1 hour.

4. Meantime, position a rack in the middle of your oven and place the Baking Steel on top. Preheat your oven to 400°F for 45 to 60 minutes.

5. Place the pans right on the preheated Baking Steel and bake for about 12 minutes or until golden on top.

6. Make the icing. Combine the confectioners' sugar and the salt in a medium bowl. Begin adding cream, starting with ¼ cup and continuing to add it, whisking the mixture, until the sugar has been absorbed and the liquid is thick but pourable. Pour over the still-hot cinnamon rolls. Sprinkle with pecan pieces, if desired. Serve warm. Store well-wrapped leftovers at room temperature for up to 2 days or freeze for up to 1 month.

DINNER ROLLS

1 recipe Brioche dough

1 egg, lightly beaten with 1 teaspoon water

1. Line a baking sheet with parchment paper.

2. Divide the dough into 12 equal portions (about 95 grams each) or any size of your liking (note that the bake time may be slightly longer or shorter depending on the

size of the rolls). Form into balls and place them on the baking sheet. Cover the sheet with plastic wrap and proof at room temperature for 2 hours.

3. Position a rack in the middle of your oven and place the Baking Steel on top. Preheat oven to 400°F for 45 to 60 minutes.

4. Brush the tops of the rolls with the egg wash and place the baking sheet on top of your preheated Baking Steel. Bake for 18 to 20 minutes or until the rolls are golden on top.

5. Store in an airtight container for up to 3 days or freeze for up to 1 month.

PULLMAN LOAF

1 recipe Brioche dough

1. Generously grease a 9-by-5-inch loaf pan.

2. Form the dough into a rectangle shape and place it in the loaf pan. Cover with lightly oiled plastic wrap and let the dough proof in the pan for about 2 hours or until it forms a "crown" over the top of the pan.

3. Position a rack in the middle of your oven and place the Baking Steel on top. Preheat oven to 400°F for 45 to 60 minutes.

4. Place the loaf pan on top of the Baking Steel and bake for 25 minutes or until the loaf is golden on top.

5. Store in an airtight container for up to 3 days or freeze for up to 1 month.

ACTUAL CORN BREAD

Here's a secret: Most corn bread is really just cake.

This, however, is actual corn bread. How can you tell? Two ways. First, it is less sweet; with just one-third cup of sugar for the whole recipe, it leaves room for the other ingredients to have an impact. Second, it contains actual kernels of corn. I have no idea why most people don't include corn in their corn bread. It's naturally sweet, it gives the bread a juicy, moist texture, and it's delicious. Ditch the extra sugar and add some kernels instead!

Putting the whole pan on top of your Baking Steel allows for even cooking, meaning that the inside is cooked through before the edges burn. And since you're the baker, you can enjoy slices as big as you like.

MAKES ONE 8-INCH-SQUARE PAN

8 tablespoons unsalted butter

62 grams (½ cup) all-purpose flour

190 grams (1½ cups) cornmeal

40 grams (⅓ cup) brown sugar

6 grams (1½ teaspoons) baking powder

1 gram (¼ teaspoon) baking soda

180 grams (1 cup) corn kernels (cut off the cob or frozen, thawed, and patted dry)

10 grams (2 teaspoons) fine sea salt

1½ cups buttermilk

1 large egg

1. Position a rack in the middle of your oven and place the Baking Steel on top. Preheat oven to 400°F for 45 to 60 minutes.

2. Meanwhile, heat the butter in a small skillet over medium heat, stirring occasionally. Once it begins to slightly darken in color, turn off the heat but continue to stir. The butter may darken a bit more and will take on a nutty aroma; milk solids will form (this is totally fine). Your butter is now browned, which will make the corn bread taste incredible. Set it aside and allow to cool.

3. In a large mixing bowl, combine the flour, cornmeal, brown sugar, baking powder, baking soda, corn kernels, and salt.

4. In a separate medium bowl, whisk together the buttermilk and egg.

5. Pour about half of the browned butter into the bottom of an 8-inch-square baking pan and tilt to thoroughly coat the pan. Pour the rest of the browned butter into the buttermilk-and-egg mixture and stir to combine.

6. Pour the liquid into the dry ingredients and stir until just combined. Pour the batter into the baking dish and tilt the pan to spread the batter. Place the pan directly on top of the hot Baking Steel and bake for 20 to 25 minutes—rotating

halfway through baking—or until a toothpick inserted in the center comes out clean.

7. Transfer to a wire rack to cool completely. Store well-wrapped leftovers at room temperature for up to 3 days or freeze for up to 1 month.

BLUEBERRY BUTTERMILK SCONES

Scones have a bad reputation, largely due to those rock-hard, triangle-shaped atrocities found at subpar chain coffee shops. But that's not the way it has to be. It's time to get sconed, and this is the recipe to take you there: blueberry scones with a great crumb, texture, and taste.

The Baking Steel works the same magic here that it does on biscuits, creating a crisp exterior and a tender, moist interior. When scones cook evenly, the edges aren't dried out by the time the inside is cooked through. But don't take my word for it; let me know what you think after you've eaten about six of these.

MAKES ABOUT 8 SCONES

550 grams (4½ cups) all-purpose flour

70 grams (½ cup) sugar, plus more for sprinkling

10 grams (2 teaspoons) fine sea salt

12 grams (1 tablespoon) baking powder

4 grams (1 teaspoon) baking soda

16 tablespoons cold unsalted butter, cut into cubes

1½ cups buttermilk, plus more for brushing the tops of the scones

135 grams (¾ cup) blueberries (or other sliced fruit; see note)

1. Position a rack in the middle of your oven and place the Baking Steel on top. Preheat oven to 400°F for 45 to 60 minutes.

CONT.

2. In a large bowl, whisk together the flour, sugar, salt, baking powder, and baking soda.

3. Add the cubed butter and press the pieces into the dry mixture using chilled hands or a pastry cutter until the mixture resembles coarse meal.

4. Add the buttermilk and blueberries and mix together until no floury bits are clinging to the sides of the bowl.

5. Turn the dough out on a floured work surface and roll into a circle approximately 1 inch thick and 12 inches across. Cut, pizza-style, into 8 wedges.

6. Place the scones on a sheet of parchment paper.

7. Brush the tops of the scones with buttermilk and sprinkle with more coarse sugar.

8. Either place your parchment on a sheet tray and put it on your Baking Steel or launch the parchment sheet directly onto your steel using a pizza peel. Bake for 13 to 15 minutes (rotating halfway through baking) or until golden on the top and sides. Remove from the Baking Steel and transfer to a wire rack to cool completely.

9. Store well-wrapped leftovers at room temperature for up to 3 days or freeze for up to 1 month.

EXTRA CREDIT **The curious case of the soggy scones.** Are you hesitant to make scones or muffins with fresh fruit because it always sinks and produces a soggy bottom? Happily, it's possible to avoid that disappointment. Simply toss the fruit briefly with a tablespoon or so of flour, just enough to give it a coating. The flour absorbs some of the fruit's moisture, which keeps the fruit afloat long enough for the baked goods to set.

LAVASH

This bread might not rise, but it will never fall flat. Lavash is a traditional Armenian flatbread made simply with a handful of ingredients. It can be rolled very thin, like a cracker, or rolled thicker for something more like naan.

Traditionally, lavash is cooked in a clay oven. But the Baking Steel is the perfect stand-in, providing a stovetop surface that can evenly and rapidly cook lavash to your liking. It also helps you get that tantalizing char on the edges of the bread that makes it such an ideal contrast to soft toppings, from hummus to cheese spread.

MAKES 1 LARGE LAVASH (8 TO 10 SERVINGS)

8 grams (2 teaspoons) toasted sesame seeds

8 grams (2 teaspoons) untoasted black sesame seeds

24 grams (2 tablespoons) toasted and ground coriander seeds

120 grams (1 cup) pastry flour

1 gram (¼ teaspoon) active dry yeast

8 grams (2 teaspoons) sugar

10 grams (2 teaspoons) fine sea salt

⅓ cup water, warm (about 105°F)

2 teaspoons olive oil, plus more for cooking

1. In a small bowl, mix together the sesame seeds and coriander. Set aside.

2. In a large bowl, combine the flour, yeast, sugar, and salt.

3. Add the warm water and olive oil; mix with a wooden spoon until combined, then knead the dough by hand until it has a smooth consistency, adding a little more water if needed. Form the dough into a ball, place in an oiled bowl, cover with a damp towel, and let rise for 1 hour.

4. Gently punch down the dough, re-cover, and let rise again for 3 more hours.

5. Turn the dough onto a lightly floured work surface. Roll out paper thin.

6. Position your Baking Steel or Baking Steel Griddle on the stovetop. Preheat on medium heat for 10 to 15 minutes, looking for a surface temperature of about 325 to 350°F.

7. From here, you can choose to make a single massive lavash or cut it into individual tortilla-chip-size portions; your choice. Brush the top or tops of the dough with oil.

8. Toast the dough, oiled-side down, on top of the Baking Steel or Baking Steel Griddle for 1 minute or until golden brown. While the first side is down, brush the top side with oil and sprinkle the spice mix on it.

CONT.

9. Flip and toast on the second side, noting that it will take less time to cook than the first side. Once done, transfer to a wire rack to cool.

10. Continue with any remaining portions of dough. Once crisp, you can store the lavash, loosely wrapped, at room temperature for up to 5 days.

EXTRA CREDIT **Be a softie!** If desired, you can make soft lavash. Simply don't roll it as thin (make it about a quarter of an inch thick); it will cook to a texture more like naan.

NAAN

In India, naan is a staple; the word translates simply to "bread." Like lavash, naan is traditionally baked in a clay oven, which gives it a crispy exterior and a fluffy interior. With the slightly charred exterior only the Baking Steel can provide, it's fantastic.

The Baking Steel Griddle allows you to attain restaurant-quality naan right on your stovetop. Make this naan and drizzle some olive oil on top for a simple snack that is second to none or serve it with cheese as an appetizer. There's nothing better.

MAKES TWELVE 6-INCH NAAN

480 grams (4 cups) all-purpose flour

65 grams (½ cup) whole-wheat flour

16 grams (1 tablespoon) fine sea salt

4 grams (1 teaspoon) baking soda

8 grams (2 teaspoons) baking powder

12 grams (1 tablespoon) sugar

2 grams (½ teaspoon) active dry yeast

1 cup buttermilk, at or slightly above room temperature

245 grams (1 cup) plain full-fat or 2-percent-milk yogurt (do not use nonfat)

Melted butter (for brushing)

1. In a large bowl, whisk together the flours, salt, baking soda, baking powder, sugar, and yeast.

2. In a separate medium bowl, combine the buttermilk and yogurt, stirring to incorporate. Pour the wet mixture into the dry ingredients. Stir with a wooden spoon until combined, then knead dough on a floured work surface with slightly wet hands (to discourage sticking) until the dough is smooth. Place the dough in a well-oiled bowl, cover with a damp, clean kitchen towel or plastic wrap, and let rise for about an hour at room temperature or until it has doubled in size.

3. Position your Baking Steel or Baking Steel Griddle on the stovetop. Preheat on medium-high heat for 10 to 15 minutes, looking for a surface temperature of about 350 to 375°F, or when a few drops of water sprinkled on the surface dance in the heat.

4. When the dough has risen, punch it down and turn it out onto a well-floured surface. Divide into 12 equal portions (about 60 grams each). Form each into a ball.

5. Roll each piece out into a thin oval approximately 6 inches long and 3 to 4 inches wide (each portion will be about ⅛ inch thick).

6. Brush each side of the naan dough with melted butter. Place the buttered dough onto your Baking Steel. Let cook for around 1 minute or until dough puffs and bubbles form on top. Check the undercarriage before flipping; it should look

CONT.

golden, with some darker spots. Flip and let the second side cook until it is crisped to your liking. Repeat with the remaining portions of dough. As you remove them from heat, stack them in a clean kitchen towel to keep them soft.

7. Store in an airtight container at room temperature for 3 to 5 days or freeze for up to 1 month.

What's the Difference Between Naan and Pita?

Plenty of people think that naan and pita are the same thing. Yes, they're both flatbreads, and when you bake them, they both puff up. Oh, and they both taste great with hummus. But they're not quite the same thing. The key differences? Acid and fat.

Naan is enriched with fat (milk, butter, or yogurt) and typically contains some sort of acid (yogurt or buttermilk). The fat makes the bread more tender; the reaction between the acid and the baking powder makes for a fluffy interior with a tender crumb.

Pita, however, is typically not enriched and depends on yeast alone for its rise. It does indeed rise, puffing dramatically like a balloon as it cooks and then flattening as it cools to give you that trademark pocket in the middle—but more about that when we get to the pita recipe.

PITA BREAD

Pita bread is always great to eat, but it's utter magic to make. For real food geeks, it's all about attaining the perfect balloon-like puff while you bake. This not only looks awesome but ensures that your pita bread will have a perfectly formed pocket once it cools.

The Baking Steel can help you nail the recipe so it looks like it came out of a commercial oven. The superhot surface allows the steam to rise through the pita, making it puff up. Once removed from the heat, the pita will slowly deflate, but you'll be left with that perfect pocket inside, ideal for filling with sandwich fixings or scooping up hummus.

MAKES EIGHT 8-INCH PITAS

420 grams (3⅓ cups) all-purpose flour

1 gram (¼ teaspoon) active dry yeast

16 grams (1 tablespoon) fine sea salt

1½ cups water, warm (about 105°F)

1. In a large bowl, combine the flour, yeast, and salt.

2. Pour in the warm water. Stir briefly to combine, then knead by hand on a lightly floured work surface for about 6 to 8 minutes (alternatively, mix for 3 to 4 minutes in a stand mixer fitted with the dough-hook attachment on medium speed) until the dough is smooth and elastic. Add a little more flour if it is too wet.

3. Transfer the mixture to an oiled bowl; cover with a damp, clean kitchen towel or plastic wrap, and let rise at room temperature for 24 hours.

4. Turn the dough onto a floured surface, and divide into 8 equal portions. Form the dough into balls, then use a rolling pin to roll the dough balls into ¼-inch-thick rounds (roughly 8 inches in diameter).

5. Let the rounds of dough rest on a lightly floured surface for 30 minutes; they will puff up slightly.

6. Meanwhile, position a rack in the middle of your oven and place the Baking Steel on top. Preheat your oven to 450°F for 45 to 60 minutes.

7. Using a pizza peel, launch the dough portions a few at a time onto your hot Baking Steel; through the oven window, watch the magic of your pita puffing up. Cook on the first side about 3 minutes, then flip using a spatula or tongs and cook for an additional 2 minutes on the second side. Repeat using the remaining portions of dough. As you remove them from the heat, stack them in a clean kitchen towel to keep them soft (they will deflate as they cool).

8. Store in an airtight container for up to 3 days at room temperature or freeze for up to 1 month.

CORN TORTILLAS

When your Baking Steel Griddle sits on top of your stove full-time, you can act as a short-order cook, delivering food on demand. One of the best and most crowd-pleasing things to whip up is corn tortillas. The possibilities are endless; from tacos to DIY tortilla chips, these are an addictive addition to your recipe arsenal.

The hot surface of the Baking Steel Griddle allows the tortilla dough to crisp on the outside almost instantly, forming a unique texture contrast with a soft interior and a slightly crisped but still flexible exterior. Serve these warm at your next build-your-own-taco night and you will win at dinner.

Note: This recipe calls for masa harina, a type of finely ground corn flour. It can usually be found in the Mexican or Hispanic section of supermarkets, or you can find it online.

MAKES ABOUT TWELVE 5- OR 6-INCH TORTILLAS

225 grams (2 cups) masa harina

10 grams (2 teaspoons) fine sea salt

1¼ cups water, warm (about 105°F)

1. Place the masa harina in a large bowl.

2. In a separate medium bowl, dissolve the salt in the warm water. Pour over the bowl of masa harina, stirring with a wooden spoon until it is combined; you're looking for a smooth but not sticky mixture.

3. Knead briefly by hand, then form the dough into a ball. Place in a lightly oiled bowl, cover with a damp towel, and let rest for 30 minutes to 2 hours.

4. Near the end of the resting period, position your Baking Steel or Baking Steel Griddle on the stovetop. Preheat on medium heat for 10 to 15 minutes, looking for a surface temperature of about 275 to 300°F, or until a few drops of water scattered on the hot surface dance when they hit the steel.

5. Grab a couple of sheets of parchment paper and a flat plate (or a tortilla press, if you happen to have one).

6. Pinch off golf-ball-size chunks of dough; roll each into a smooth ball. Set between two pieces of parchment and flatten a bit with your hand. Press down using a plate or a tortilla press to flatten the dough into a traditional tortilla shape. Remove the plate or press and peel back the parchment paper. Repeat with the remaining portions; you can reuse the parchment paper.

7. Transfer the rounds of dough, a few at a time, to the prepared Baking Steel, making sure that each has enough space so that they don't stick together.

8. Cook for about 2 minutes on each side, keeping in mind that the second side will take slightly less time to cook than the first. As you remove the tortillas, stack them in a clean kitchen towel to keep them soft.

9. Store leftovers in an airtight container in the refrigerator for 3 to 5 days or freeze for up to 1 month.

EXTRA CREDIT Make them into crispy tortilla shells!

CRISPY TORTILLA SHELLS

Many taco purists will tell you that soft taco shells are the only way to go. But sometimes you crave something crispy. Happily, it's easy to transform these homemade corn tortillas into crispy shells; just follow these steps.

1. Remove the tortilla from the Baking Steel and lightly form it into a taco shape with your hands. Do this right after removing it from heat, when it is still fairly flexible.

2. Place a small piece of scrunched-up aluminum foil in its center so that it will keep its shape.

3. Repeat with the remaining tortillas you want to make crispy.

4. With the foil still in place to keep them open, toast the shells on the still-hot Baking Steel until they have crisped.

5. Fill them with the taco toppings of your choice.

Alternatively, after making tortillas, you can slice them into slivers and toast them on the Baking Steel Griddle with a little olive oil for easy DIY tortilla chips!

SOFT PRETZELS

As a dad, I've put in plenty of time at my kids' hockey games. Without fail, after every game, both of my sons want to indulge in the rink food court's pretzels. They are not good, so we came up with our own recipe. To the uninitiated, making pretzels seems complicated, but it's actually a pretty easy way to learn the basics of bread making. You use a simple dough that comes together in minutes, and the rest of the process is similar to making bagels: shape, submerge, bake, snack.

Pretzels, unlike bagels, aren't boiled; it might sound strange, but they are poached in a solution of water and baking soda. The alkaline water makes the dough slightly gummy, which helps ensure that the baked pretzels will have a chewy interior and an outer crust browned to perfection.

This recipe gives you instructions for how to make classic soft pretzels, but you can also use the dough to make soft-pretzel buns, which are perfect for sandwiches or burgers.

MAKES 6 MEDIUM PRETZELS OR 12 PRETZEL BUNS

480 grams (4 cups) all-purpose flour

12 grams (1 tablespoon) confectioners' sugar

10 grams (2 teaspoons) fine sea salt

2 grams (½ teaspoon) active dry yeast

1½ cups water, warm (about 105°F)

4 tablespoons unsalted butter, melted

For the poaching mixture

8 cups water

72 grams (¼ cup) baking soda

To top

Pretzel salt

Melted butter, for serving (optional)

1. In the bowl of a stand mixer fitted with the dough hook, combine the flour, sugar, salt, and yeast.

2. With the mixer running on low, slowly add the warm water; mix briefly to incorporate.

3. Add the melted butter and mix on medium speed for about 4 minutes. The dough will form a loose ball and pull away from the sides of the bowl.

4. Transfer the dough to an oiled bowl, cover with a clean, damp kitchen towel or plastic wrap, and let rise at room temperature for up to an hour. The dough will expand to a little more than double its original size.

5. Meanwhile, position a rack in the middle of your oven and place the Baking Steel on top. Preheat oven to 450°F for 45 to 60 minutes.

CONT.

6. Turn the risen dough onto a floured work surface. Divide the dough into 6 equal portions (about 145 grams each) for pretzels or 12 equal portions (about 70 grams each) for buns. Shape each portion into a pretzel (see opposite) or form them into balls (page 166) to make pretzel buns.

7. Prepare the poaching mixture. Bring the water and baking soda to a boil; once the baking soda is dissolved, turn off the heat.

8. Using your hands, drop your pretzels into the poaching solution and let sit for about 10 to 15 seconds; flip with tongs, and repeat on the second side. Be careful; the mixture is hot and can stain your clothes if it splatters. Remove the pretzels with a slotted spoon so that the excess liquid can drain off and place them on a sheet of parchment paper. Coat generously with pretzel salt. Then either place your parchment on a sheet tray and put that on your Baking Steel, or use a pizza peel to launch the parchment directly onto your Baking Steel.

9. Bake for 10 to 12 minutes (rotating halfway through baking) or until golden brown; they will take the same amount of time to cook whether you've shaped them into pretzels or rolls. Remove from the Baking Steel and transfer to a wire rack to cool. If you want, brush the pretzels with melted butter when you take them out for added flavor!

10. Store well-wrapped leftovers for up to 3 days or freeze for up to 1 month.

EXTRA CREDIT **What is pretzel salt?** Pretzel salt is a coarse, large-grained salt that doesn't melt quickly. Because it's sturdier than typical coarse salt or even flaky sea salt, it's the perfect choice for finishing salt bagels, bread sticks, or pretzels. If it is not available in your grocery store, use the coarsest salt you can find.

How to Shape Pretzels

It may look like origami folding, but shaping pretzels couldn't be simpler. Here's how to do it in four easy steps.

1. Roll the dough into a long, slender log. About 14 inches is a good length for this recipe.

2. Gather the dough into a horseshoe shape with the ends of the U pointed down.

3. Overlap the ends, leaving approximately 2-inch tails, so it kind of looks like a ribbon symbol. You can coil once or twice more if desired.

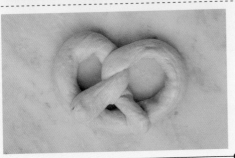

4. Flip the overlapping ends down so that they meet the bottom of the rounded part. You'll see the familiar pretzel shape appear. If the circles are too tight, use your fingers to widen the holes for a more pleasing pretzel shape.

HAMBURGER BUNS

In my opinion, the bun plays a vital supporting role to the burger. It should be soft, so your teeth can go right to the main event. It should be absorbent but not so spongy that it becomes gooey and wet when you give it a squeeze.

This enriched dough has enough milk and melted butter to keep the buns soft and tender. Potato flour keeps them moist. Baking them on the Baking Steel ensures even and quick baking so they can perfectly set on the top and bottom and get tender and soft on the inside but will remain sturdy enough to hold your burger without getting soggy. These are the perfect buns for making Ultra-Smashed Cheeseburgers (page 210).

MAKES 12 BUNS

360 grams (2¾ cups) all-purpose flour	1½ cups milk, warm
50 grams (½ cup) potato flour	4 tablespoons melted butter
5 grams (1 teaspoon) fine sea salt	2 tablespoons honey
2 grams (½ teaspoon) active dry yeast	1 large egg, lightly beaten with 1 teaspoon water

DAY 1

1. In a large bowl, combine the flours, salt, and yeast; give the mixture a quick stir with a wooden spoon to combine.

2. Add the milk, melted butter, and honey to the bowl. Mix together with a wooden spoon until thoroughly combined, then knead by hand on a well-floured work surface for 6 to 8 minutes (alternatively, you can mix for 3 to 4 minutes on medium speed in a stand mixer fitted with the dough-hook attachment) to form a smooth, soft, sticky dough. It should be easy to form into a ball.

3. Transfer to a lightly oiled bowl, cover with a clean, damp kitchen towel or plastic wrap, and let sit at room temperature for 24 hours.

DAY 2

4. Turn the dough out onto a work surface and divide into 12 equal portions (about 85 grams each). Shape into balls.

5. Place the balls, seam-side down, on a lined sheet tray. Cover with plastic and proof on the baking sheet for 2 hours.

6. About halfway through the proofing period, place your Baking Steel on the middle rack in your oven. Preheat oven to 350°F for 45 to 60 minutes.

7. Brush the rolls with the egg wash.

8. Place the baking sheet on top of the Baking Steel.

9. Bake for 16 to 18 minutes (rotating halfway through baking) or until golden on top.

10. Remove the baking sheet from the oven and place the buns on a wire rack to cool completely.

11. Store well-wrapped leftovers at room temperature for up to 3 days or freeze for up to 1 month.

MULTIGRAIN BREAD LOAF

This recipe combines the revolutionary powers of steel with the baking properties of a Dutch oven. Because of the Dutch oven's sturdy walls, it can be used both on the stovetop and in the oven, and it is well suited for low-and-slow cooking methods. In this recipe, the Dutch oven traps condensation inside it while the bread bakes, giving it a chewier, firmer crust. The conductivity of the Baking Steel ensures that the bread bakes perfectly on the top and all the way through to support that stellar crust.

MAKES ONE 9-INCH LOAF

400 grams (3¼ cups) bread flour

130 grams (1 cup) multigrain whole-wheat flour

16 grams (1 tablespoon) fine sea salt

1 gram (¼ teaspoon) active dry yeast

1¼ cups water, warm (about 105°F)

2 tablespoons honey

Special equipment

4½-quart (about 9-inch-diameter) Dutch oven

1. In a large mixing bowl, whisk together the dry ingredients.

2. Add the warm water and honey and mix with a wooden spoon just to combine. Turn the dough out on a well-floured work surface and knead by hand for about 6 to 8 minutes. (Alternatively, you can mix for 3 to 4 minutes on medium speed in a stand mixer fitted with the dough-hook attachment until the dough is elastic and pulling away from the sides of the bowl.) Add more flour if it is too wet.

3. Place in a lightly oiled bowl and cover with a clean, damp kitchen towel or plastic wrap. Let rise at room temperature for 24 hours.

4. Turn the dough out onto a floured surface and shape into a round loaf. Cover with a damp, clean kitchen towel and let rise at room temperature for 2 hours.

5. Position your Baking Steel on a rack in the lower-middle part of your oven. Place the Dutch oven, with the lid on, on the steel and preheat at 400°F for 45 to 60 minutes.

6. Using a bread *lame* or a sharp razor blade, make three diagonal slashes or a crisscross pattern on top of the loaf.

7. Carefully remove the hot Dutch oven and place on a heatproof surface. Remove the lid. Working quickly and cautiously, pick up the dough and place it in the

Dutch oven. Cover it, place the Dutch oven back in the oven, and cook, covered, for 25 minutes. Remove the lid and continue to cook for 10 to 12 additional minutes.

8. Remove the Dutch oven and place it on a wire rack to cool completely before removing the bread. Store leftovers in a paper bag for up to 3 days or freeze for up to 1 month.

NOTE: If you don't have a Dutch oven, it's well worth the investment to get one. But if today isn't the day, you can also shape the loaf free-form and bake directly on the Baking Steel. Just give it a spritz of water using a spray bottle before you close the oven door.

SEEDED BREAD

Some people like their bread with minimal mix-ins; others like to jam as many seeds, nuts, and grains into their bread as they possibly can. This loaf is for the latter group. It's got a symphony of textures and flavors that work with just about anything you want to use it for, from grilled cheese to French toast. Plus, with its myriad of seeds dotting the top and inside of each slice, it's a beautiful bread for Instagram shots.

While seeded breads are notorious for having a dry texture, the evenly distributed heat of the Baking Steel's surface produces a seed-studded loaf with a moist interior.

MAKES ONE 9-BY-5-INCH LOAF

42 grams (3 tablespoons) raw pumpkin seeds

28 grams (2 tablespoons) raw sunflower seeds

28 grams (2 tablespoons) millet seeds

14 grams (1 tablespoon) poppy seeds

240 grams (2 cups) bread flour

160 grams (1¼ cups) whole-wheat flour

16 grams (1 tablespoon) fine sea salt

2 grams (½ teaspoon) active dry yeast

4 tablespoons honey

2 tablespoons dark molasses

1¼ cups water, warm (about 105°F)

2 tablespoons olive oil

DAY 1

1. In a medium bowl, combine the seeds.

2. In a large bowl, combine the flours, salt, yeast, and half the seed mixture. Stir briefly to combine, then add the honey, molasses, water, and olive oil. Stir to moisten the dry ingredients, then knead for about 6 to 8 minutes by hand (alternatively, 3 to 4 minutes using a stand mixer fitted with the dough-hook attachment) until the dough is elastic and forms a smooth ball.

3. Transfer the dough to a lightly oiled bowl, cover with a clean, damp kitchen towel or plastic wrap, and let sit at room temperature for 24 hours.

DAY 2

4. Punch down the dough, and gather the corners in toward the center. Remove the dough from the bowl and shape into a log. Place the dough, seam-side down, in an oiled 9-by-5-inch loaf pan. Let it proof at room temperature for 2 hours.

5. About halfway through the proofing period, position a rack in the middle of your oven and place the Baking Steel on top. Preheat oven to 350°F for 45 to 60 minutes.

6. Brush the top of loaf with a small amount of water (just enough to make it sticky) and sprinkle the remainder of the seed mixture on top.

7. Place the loaf pan directly on top of the Baking Steel. Bake the bread for 25 minutes, rotating halfway through baking. I like to knock on the top of it when I think it's about done; if it is, it will have a slightly hollow sound. When the bread is done, remove it from the oven and place on a wire rack to cool.

8. Store in a paper bag for up to 3 days at room temperature or freeze for up to 1 month.

4

BEYOND
BAKING

EXPLORING THE CAPABILITIES OF THE BAKING STEEL

When I started with the Baking Steel project, my goal was to deliver "the crust you crave" to customers. Nailed it; the Baking Steel can turn a standard home oven into an industrial powerhouse by reaching temperatures higher than 700 degrees Fahrenheit, perfect for creating pizza and bread crusts rivaling those baked in commercial ovens. But as I have discovered along the way, the Baking Steel is capable of much more.

Our second major product release, the Baking Steel Griddle, opened up new avenues of cooking and baking with steel. One side is the same as the traditional Baking Steel: slightly textured and ideal for putting right in the oven to make perfect pizza and bread. On the flip side, the Baking Steel Griddle has a flat, smooth surface and a channel along the perimeter to capture grease. These touches allow you to take the Baking Steel Griddle out of your oven and use it on your stovetop...and beyond. We toyed with this tool in the bread chapter, but now we're really going to dig in; I'll show you how, using both of these Baking Steel surfaces, you can upgrade every meal, from breakfast to dinner. Of course, many of the stovetop recipes can also be prepared using a traditional Baking Steel surface; in the cases where the Baking Steel Griddle really is the best tool, I've made note of it in the recipe heading.

You can create a DIY diner-style range by placing the griddle directly on your stovetop, grill perfect burgers with your steel atop the grates of your outdoor grill, or even freeze it down with dry ice to make ice cream in moments—this slab of steel goes far beyond the capabilities of a pizza stone or skillet. This chapter will open up a world of possibilities for making delicious, restaurant-caliber food with this truly unique cooking tool.

BREAKFAST

LIGHT AND FLUFFY PANCAKES
WITH CHINESE SAUSAGE

Pancakes or sausage? Why choose one? This clever and inventive recipe, dreamed up by Jenn Louis (the culinary genius who brought you the stromboli in the pizza chapter), allows you to enjoy them in one fluffy, sweet-and-savory form. You place the sausage on the hot griddle and then pour the batter right over it, so the sausage cooks right into the pancakes. These pancakes feature Chinese sausage, which is already cured, so all you have to do is sear the slices before you pour the batter over them. The result? Tender, fluffy pancakes studded with savory sausage that will make you a breakfast or brunch superstar.

MAKES 8 LARGE PANCAKES

260 grams (2 cups) all-purpose flour

36 grams (3 tablespoons) sugar

4 grams (1 teaspoon) kosher salt

24 grams (2 tablespoons) baking powder

2 large eggs, separated

4 tablespoons unsalted butter, melted

1¾ cups whole milk

Vegetable oil

8 links Chinese sausage, sliced into ½-inch rounds (see note)

Butter and maple syrup, to serve

1. Whisk together the flour, sugar, salt, and baking powder in a large bowl. Set aside.

2. In a separate large bowl or in a stand mixer fitted with the whisk attachment, beat the egg whites until stiff peaks form. Set aside.

3. Stir the egg yolks, melted butter, and milk into the flour mixture, then use a spatula to fold in the whipped egg whites.

4. Position your Baking Steel Griddle on the stovetop. Preheat on medium-high heat for about 10 to 15 minutes for a surface temperature of 300 to 350°F. You can test the surface by sprinkling a drop or two of vegetable oil on it; the oil should immediately begin sizzling.

5. Pour a teaspoon or so of vegetable oil on the Baking Steel Griddle, then place a small handful of sliced Chinese sausage on the hot surface.

6. Pour half a cup of the pancake batter over the sausage and let cook until bubbles form on top of the pancake and the sides start to cook, about 3 minutes. Flip the pancake to finish cooking, then repeat with the remaining sausage and batter. If at any point the pan becomes dry, add a small drizzle of oil.

7. Serve immediately with butter and maple syrup.

EXTRA CREDIT **What is Chinese sausage?** Jenn uses a type called *lap xuong*, small-link, marinated, smoked pork sausages with an assertive, fatty flavor. If you are unable to find Chinese sausage where you live, you can make these pancakes with small slices of your favorite sausage, cooked and cooled (or you can use a precooked variety).

FRENCH TOAST

Mediocre French toast is easy to come by; it's served in diners and kitchens everywhere. Excellent French toast, however, is a bit more elusive. The Baking Steel Griddle, paired with the proper technique and ingredients, can help you attain that certain *je ne sais quoi*.

Using an absorbent bread is key here. Slices of brioche, my favorite for French toast, act like little sponges, absorbing the custardy mixture of milk, egg, and spices. The moment these saturated slices hit the heated surface of your steel griddle, they will begin to set, sealing that creamy texture on the inside while allowing for a perfect golden-brown, crispy outside.

MAKES 4 THICK SLICES

2 large eggs

½ cup whole milk

2 grams (1 teaspoon) ground cinnamon

Pinch each (or to taste) of ground clove, ginger, and nutmeg

4 (1 inch thick) slices day-old bread (we suggest Brioche, page 145)

4 tablespoons unsalted butter, melted

Suggested garnishes: fruit, butter, confectioners' sugar, maple syrup

1. Position your Baking Steel or Baking Steel Griddle on the stovetop. Preheat on medium-high heat for 10 to 15 minutes for a surface temperature of 275 to 300°F. If you place a small pat of butter on the surface, it should begin bubbling gently but should not brown or blacken right away.

2. Whisk together the eggs, milk, and spices in a shallow bowl or pie plate.

3. Soak the bread slices in the wet mixture, pressing on the bread to make sure all the liquid gets fully absorbed.

4. Brush some of the melted butter on the surface of the hot Baking Steel.

5. Place the bread down on top of the butter; you want to hear a little sizzle, but not too much. You're not trying to sear the toast over super-high heat; it's more of a slow-and-steady approach.

6. After about 1 to 2 minutes, lift a corner of the bread with a spatula. If the bread looks browned to your liking, flip to cook the second side.

7. Once toasted to your liking, remove the slices from the Baking Steel.

8. Garnish as you see fit; serve immediately.

KITCHEN-SINK BREAKFAST

When I was seventeen, I was a short-order cook at Pancake King. My domain? The griddle. On Sunday mornings, we served up to three hundred folks over the course of two hours. If you needed a break, too bad. Fast-forward thirty years and I'm in the same role, only the guests are my kids and the griddle is of the Baking Steel variety. The large Baking Steel Griddle spans two burners on the stovetop, which means that I have plenty of room to cook multiple breakfast items on it concurrently. Our mini-version of the Baking Steel Griddle won't allow you the same amount of room, but you can still get the job done.

Some short-order tips for the uninitiated: Always start with what is going to take the longest to cook. In this case, it's the potatoes. You'll cover the entire Baking Steel Griddle with your little spuds and let them cook until tender, then you'll move them to the side to keep warm. You'll cook your bacon for two to three minutes on each side before removing. Have your eggs at the ready, and start taking orders. Cook the eggs on the hot front of the griddle, and keep those potatoes warming on the back. As the eggs cook, slice your bread; toss the slices on the still-hot griddle, and you'll have toast in seconds. Plate everything up, and breakfast is served.

MAKES 4 SERVINGS

CHEESY POTATOES

4 tablespoons olive oil

900 grams (2 pounds) russet potatoes, cut into ½-inch cubes

Onion powder

Fine sea salt and pepper

50 to 100 grams (1 to 2 slices) good melting cheese, such as Cheddar or provolone

1. Position your Baking Steel Griddle on the stovetop. Preheat for about 10 to 15 minutes on medium heat, looking for a surface temperature of 300 to 350°F. You can test the surface by sprinkling a small amount of olive oil on it; the droplets should begin bubbling assertively.

2. Coat the surface of the Baking Steel Griddle with olive oil, then carefully place the potatoes on top.

3. Season the potatoes with onion powder, salt, and pepper. Allow them to sear, then start flipping them around on the surface using a metal spatula. Continue to cook, shuffling them frequently, for about 20 to 30 minutes, or until crisped to your liking.

CONT.

4. Place the cheese on top of your hot potatoes. Using your spatula, flip the potatoes around in the melting cheese until each cube is well coated.

5. Once the cheese has melted, shift the potatoes to a portion of the griddle farthest away from the burner so they can stay warm but won't overcook while you prepare the remaining items. If using the mini-griddle, move the potatoes to a bowl and cover with a towel to keep warm.

BACON

12 slices bacon (store-bought or make your own, page 194)

1. With the Cheesy Potatoes off to the side, add your bacon to the still-hot griddle.

2. Cook for 2 to 3 minutes per side, turning when crisped to your liking.

3. Remove from the griddle and transfer to a serving platter while you prepare the eggs.

NOTE: You can substitute any other breakfast meat and follow the same basic method.

FRIED EGGS

8 eggs
Butter or olive oil

1. Reduce the heat of the Baking Steel Griddle to about 275°F; to test the surface, sprinkle a small amount of olive oil on top of it; it should begin bubbling gently.

2. Since you just cooked your meat, chances are, you have some grease left over on the surface of the still-hot Baking Steel Griddle. You can use just this to keep the eggs from sticking, or you can add some butter or oil to the surface to make sure that it's generously greased.

3. Crack the eggs right onto the Baking Steel Griddle; they should begin to bubble around the edges fairly quickly. Sliding a spatula under the egg should be easy if the griddle is well oiled.

4. For sunny-side-up eggs, remove the eggs when the whites are set; for over-easy eggs, as soon as the whites are set, gently flip the eggs over and cook briefly (about 15 to 20 seconds).

TOAST

8 slices bread

1. With the Baking Steel Griddle surface temperature still hovering at about 275°F, add a little more reserved bacon grease or a nice pat of butter to the surface, then lay a piece of bread on top.

2. Toast until evenly browned on the first side, then flip and brown the second side to match. Repeat with as many slices as you need for your hungry crowd.

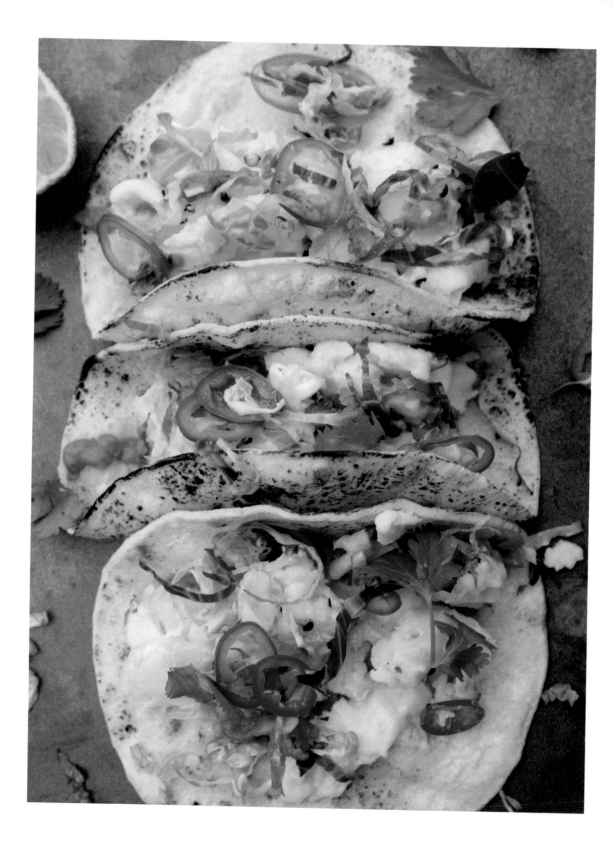

BREAKFAST TACOS

Who says tacos should be consumed only after noon? Start your Taco Tuesday (or, really, any day) off right, bright and early, by making breakfast tacos.

This recipe takes both tacos and breakfast to a new level. These naturally gluten-free delights start with homemade corn tortillas that you fill with a protein-rich and energizing mixture of perfectly scrambled eggs and a tangy brussels sprout slaw, accented with a generous dollop of Green Chile Sauce.

MAKES 5 TACOS

113 grams (4 ounces) brussels sprouts, shaved crosswise on a mandoline or thinly sliced

1 sweet Italian red pepper, sliced

4 tablespoons apple cider vinegar

2 tablespoons olive oil

Fine sea salt and pepper

5 Corn Tortillas (page 162)

3 large eggs

¾ cup Green Chile Sauce (page 204)

1. Make the brussels sprout slaw: In a large mixing bowl, toss the brussels sprouts and red pepper slices with the apple cider vinegar, olive oil, and salt and pepper. Set aside.

2. Line a wire rack with parchment paper. Heat the Baking Steel Griddle on medium-high heat for 10 to 15 minutes for a surface temperature of 275 to 300°F. To test the surface, sprinkle a few drops of water on it; they should dance on the hot steel.

3. Place a tortilla on the griddle to warm and color. Cook for about 2 minutes; flip and repeat on the second side. Set aside. Repeat with the remaining tortillas.

4. Reduce heat to medium-low. Crack the eggs right on top of the griddle and, using your spatula, make karate chop–like movements to keep them in gentle motion as they scramble. Cook the eggs until done to your liking. Remove from the hot surface.

5. To assemble, fill the tortillas with eggs, slaw, Green Chile Sauce. Serve immediately.

QUICK AND EASY HASH BROWNS

In my house, hash browns are nearly always part of the artful breakfast splayed across my Baking Steel Griddle in the morning. The hot surface of the steel ensures that they attain the perfect crust while baking evenly all over—think golden everywhere, not undercooked in one area and blackened in another.

MAKES SIX 3-INCH PATTIES

900 grams (2 pounds) russet potatoes, peeled and grated

Fine sea salt and pepper

1 sweet Italian red pepper, thinly sliced

56 grams (2 ounces) scallions, thinly sliced

8 tablespoons unsalted butter, melted

1. Position your Baking Steel Griddle on the stovetop. Preheat on medium-high for 10 to 15 minutes; you're looking for a surface temperature of 325 to 350°F. To test the surface, sprinkle a small amount of butter on it; it should begin to bubble assertively but should not turn brown or black.

2. Place the grated potatoes in a large bowl. Season with salt and pepper to taste, then mix in the peppers and scallions. Make sure that everything is evenly distributed.

3. Using your hands, form the potato mixture into 6 patties about 3 inches across.

4. Brush the griddle liberally with melted butter.

5. Place the patties on top of the buttered griddle. Cook until deep golden brown on the bottom, about 3 to 4 minutes, then flip with a metal spatula. If patties are beginning to stick, brush the surface with more melted butter as needed. Cook for an additional 2 to 3 minutes or until the second side is toasted to your liking.

6. Remove and transfer to a serving platter. Serve immediately.

DIY PERFECT BACON

The Baking Steel Griddle can help you cook the best bacon you've ever had in your life. The only way to enhance this culinary experience? Use the best bacon you've ever tasted in your life. For me, that bacon is the homemade variety.

File this under *mind-blowing*: You can make your own bacon. And let me tell you, it's a thing of salty beauty. It's surprisingly easy to make and doesn't call for any hard-to-find ingredients or complicated techniques. While a smoker will infuse your bacon with added flavor, it's not necessary.

You'll be wowed by how much better the homemade stuff is; it's even better than the high-end bacon in the supermarket. You'll be even more wowed when you taste this perfect bacon fresh off the Baking Steel Griddle.

MAKES 12 TO 16 SLICES PER POUND OF PORK BELLY

4 pounds pork belly, skin on

50 grams (¼ cup) kosher salt

8 grams (2 teaspoons) pink curing salt (see recipe note)

50 grams (¼ cup) packed dark brown sugar

¼ cup maple syrup

8 grams (2 tablespoons) crushed red pepper flakes

8 grams (2 tablespoons) smoked sweet paprika

4 grams (1 teaspoon) coriander seeds

4 grams (1 teaspoon) cumin seeds

1. Rinse the pork belly and dry with towel. Place belly in a Pyrex or other type of high-sided pan large enough to fit it without folding.

2. Mix all salts, sugar, syrup, and spices in a bowl. Coat the pork belly all over with the mixture.

3. Wrap belly tightly in plastic wrap and refrigerate for 6 to 8 days, flipping the belly over once a day.

4. Remove the belly from the plastic wrap (you should see a lot of liquid at the bottom of the dish). Clean the dish and dry it thoroughly. Rinse the belly off and put it back in the clean container in the refrigerator for 2 days to air-dry. Use a Pyrex container and keep it covered very loosely. (We need the bacon to dry, so cover it loosely for sanitary reasons but don't wrap it up tight.)

5. Preheat your oven to 250°F. Cover the belly loosely in foil and cook on a roasting rack over a rimmed baking sheet for 2 to 3 hours or until it reaches an internal temperature of 148 to 152°F. If you have a home smoker, cook in your smoker to the same temperature.

6. Once cooked or smoked but while it's still warm, place the back of a sheet tray on top of the belly (still wrapped in tinfoil) and weight it with a heavy object. Once the belly is cool, transfer the whole thing, still weighted down, to the refrigerator and keep overnight to shape flat. Once flattened, you can cook the bacon immediately or store in the refrigerator for up to 3 days before using.

7. When you're ready to cook, slice the belly lengthwise into strips. Typically, you'll get 12 to 16 slices per pound of pork belly when cutting a sixteenth of an inch per slice, but sometimes I like to cut it a bit thicker.

8. To cook the bacon, position your Baking Steel Griddle on the stovetop. Preheat for 10 to 15 minutes on medium heat, for a surface temperature of 300 to 325°F. To test the surface, sprinkle a few drops of water on it; they should dance on the hot steel.

9. Place the bacon on the hot Baking Steel Griddle and cook for 2 to 3 minutes or until crisped to your liking. Flip and cook the second side. Remove from the griddle and transfer to paper towels to cool. Blot excess oil before serving.

NOTE: Curing salt is available in the spice aisle in many grocery stores. You may see it marked as TCM or Tinted Curing Mixture, also known as pink salt.

LUNCH AND DINNER

GRILLED CHEESE

Have you ever noticed that a grilled cheese sandwich from a diner always tastes amazing? That's because short-order cooks at diners use large, flat griddle surfaces. The heat permeates the sandwich inside and out, allowing for the perfect browning of the bread while leaving the inside of the sandwich gooey, cheesy, and perfect.

The Baking Steel Griddle's flat surface area and even heat allow you to attain that toasty, cheesy perfection at home, but you'll do it using higher-quality ingredients than the diner does. Break out the tomato soup to pair with this better-than-childhood version of a classic sandwich.

MAKES 1 SANDWICH

2 slices white bread

4 tablespoons unsalted butter, softened

60 grams (2 ounces) Muenster, sliced

60 grams (2 ounces) fresh mozzarella, sliced

Optional add-ins: thinly sliced tomato, ham, apple slices, or whatever you'd like

1. Position your Baking Steel on the stovetop. Preheat on medium-high for 10 to 15 minutes for a surface temperature of 300 to 325°F. To test the surface, place a small amount of butter on it; it should begin to bubble assertively but should not turn brown or black.

2. Aggressively butter one side of each slice of bread with your softened butter.

3. Place one slice of bread, butter-side down, on the griddle. Layer the top with cheese. If you want to add slices of tomato, ham, or other ingredients, be sure to sandwich them between layers of cheese. Top with the second slice, butter-side up.

4. Cook the first side for about 2 minutes or until golden and crispy. Flip with a metal spatula and cook the second side until it's equally crispy and the cheese is perfectly melty. Remove from the griddle and enjoy immediately.

CHICKEN PARMESAN SANDWICH

While chicken Parm is often relegated to the category of "things that I buy" rather than "things that I make," it's surprisingly easy and quick to cook at home. Butterflied chicken breasts are given an SBP (standard breading procedure), then thrown on the griddle. The heat absorbed by the inner core of the steel during preheating ensures that the chicken is cooked to golden perfection, sealing in the juicy interior while producing a crunchy crust on the outside.

Served on a buttered bun, toasted concurrently with the sandwich, then topped with homemade tomato sauce and gooey mozzarella, this is a satisfying meal indeed.

MAKES 1 SANDWICH

56 grams (½ cup) all-purpose flour, seasoned with a pinch of salt and pepper

1 large egg, whisked with 1 teaspoon water

20 grams (4 tablespoons) panko bread crumbs

1 6-ounce boneless, skinless chicken breast, butterflied (see opposite)

4 tablespoons honey mustard

2 teaspoons olive oil

½ cup tomato sauce

Butter, softened

1 soft kaiser roll

113 grams (4 ounces) mozzarella, thinly sliced

Fresh basil (optional)

1. Position your Baking Steel Griddle on the stovetop. Preheat on medium-high heat for 10 to 15 minutes, looking for a surface temperature of 300 to 325°F.

2. Set up 3 separate bowls, one with the flour, one with the egg wash, and one with the panko. Set them up in that order, with the panko bowl closest to the griddle.

3. Rub the chicken all over with the honey mustard.

4. Dip the chicken first in the flour, then in the egg wash, then in the bread crumbs.

5. Brush the Baking Steel Griddle with olive oil and place the chicken on the oiled surface. Cook the first side for about 3 minutes or until deep golden and toasty. Flip and cook on the second side; note that it may take slightly less time to cook than the first side.

6. Near the end of the cooking time, heat your tomato sauce and butter both halves of your roll. Place the roll, butter-side down, on the griddle and toast to your liking.

7. On the bottom bun, stack the chicken, sauce, cheese, another layer of sauce, and the top bun. If you'd like, you can add some basil too. Serve immediately.

Steel + Butterfly = A Marriage Made in Meat Heaven

The Baking Steel ensures even cooking. Butterflying is a method of creating a uniform thickness in your meat by slicing it and opening it like a butterfly's wings (hence the name). With the power of uniform thickness combined with even cooking, you end up with perfect chicken, steak, or whatever you've butterflied every time. Here's a quick-and-dirty three-step guide on how to butterfly:

1. Place your chicken breast on a chopping board. Holding it steady with one hand, use a sharp knife to slice into one side of the breast, starting at the thickest part and ending at the thinnest. Don't cut all the way through.

2. Open the breast like the pages of a book. (Or, you know, like butterfly wings.)

3. Cover with plastic wrap or place in a Ziploc bag and whack a few times with a mallet or rolling pin to pound to an even thickness. Proceed with your recipe.

BLT

This BLT is a thing of beauty. Juicy tomatoes are the beating heart of this sandwich, but it's the supporting cast of crispy bacon, soft bread, iceberg lettuce, and mayonnaise that gives it soul. A BLT might seem like extremely humble fare, but when it's made with quality ingredients and prepared well, it's perfection. This is the type of thing that four-star chefs eat on their days off.

The Baking Steel Griddle helps make this sandwich a standout by providing the sizzling surface to cook your bacon to perfection. After you cook the bacon, you toast your bread in the residual bacon fat, which infuses it with flavor. Pile on the rest of the ingredients and take a bite; you may never look at a BLT the same way again.

MAKES 1 SANDWICH

100 grams (4 strips) bacon (you can make your own [page 194], but store-bought will do)

2 slices potato or White Bread (page 143)

2 tablespoons mayonnaise

150 grams (3 large slices) heirloom tomato

Fine sea salt and pepper

3 to 4 outer leaves of lettuce (I prefer iceberg)

1. Position your Baking Steel Griddle on the stovetop. Preheat on medium-high for 10 to 15 minutes, looking for a surface temperature of 300 to 325°F.

2. Add the bacon to the Baking Steel Griddle and cook for 2 to 3 minutes per side or until crisped to your liking. Remove and place on paper towels set above a wire rack to cool.

3. Place the bread on top of the still-hot steel and allow it to toast in the bacon fat. Once it's toasted to your liking on the first side, flip and toast the second side to match.

4. Lay both slices of toast side by side and spread the mayonnaise on top. Place the bacon on top of just one of the slices.

5. Season the tomato slices on both sides with salt and pepper to taste. Place the slices on top of the bread with the bacon. Lay the lettuce on the bacon, then place the second slice of bread, mayonnaise-side down, on top. You can slice it if you want, but nobody's judging you if you want to dig right in. Serve immediately.

GREEN CHILE CHICKEN DRUMSTICKS

Living in the seaside town of Cohasset, Massachusetts, I have ample opportunity for entertaining in the outdoors during the warmer months. When it's time to cook, my Baking Steel Griddle goes outside with me.

The griddle can actually be put right on top of your outdoor grill or set up on a couple of cinder blocks with Sterno underneath for easy outdoor cooking. If you don't have outdoor space, you can cook these on the stovetop. Regardless of your heat source, the chicken drumsticks cook quickly and evenly on the griddle, which produces a crispy crust that seals in the flavor. Tossed in an addictive Green Chile Sauce and garnished with cotija cheese, cilantro, and toasted sunflower seeds, these are the perfect food to savor in the summer, but they're just as good any other time of year.

MAKES 20 DRUMSTICKS

20 chicken drumsticks, as is or frenched (see technique note below)

2 to 3 tablespoons olive oil

Fine sea salt and pepper

1½ cups Green Chile Sauce (recipe follows)

125 grams (4 ounces) cotija cheese, grated

60 grams (2 ounces) cilantro, whole leaves

30 grams (1 ounce) sunflower seeds, toasted

1. Heat your griddle to medium-high heat on the stovetop, grill top, or on top of two cans of Sterno for 10 to 15 minutes for a surface temperature of 300 to 325°F.

2. Coat the drumsticks in oil, then sprinkle liberally with salt and pepper.

3. Arrange the drumsticks on the griddle so that they are not touching one another.

4. Keep turning the drumsticks every few minutes, making sure to get great color all over. They'll take about 16 minutes total to cook through.

5. Once you are happy with the doneness of the drumsticks, throw them in a mixing bowl with the Green Chile Sauce, cotija cheese, cilantro, and sunflower seeds. Toss to coat evenly, and serve.

EXTRA CREDIT Let's go French. I like to prepare this recipe with chicken drums that are frenched, which means the tough tissues along the bottom bone portion are removed. Not only does this make for a nice presentation but it helps the chicken cook more evenly and prevents the coarse skin over the bone from sticking to the pan. To french your chicken drumsticks, cut around just below the handle of the drums to separate the skin. With the heel of a chef's knife, cut through the knuckle of the chicken bone. You should be able to just move the small amount of skin off the bone and be left with a clean cut. Now your drumsticks are perfectly prepared to cook evenly on the hot Baking Steel Griddle.

GREEN CHILE SAUCE

While this sauce is intended as a coating for the drumsticks in the recipe above, you may find that it's one of those sauces that you'll want to put on everything. Luckily, it comes together in minutes, making it easy to whip up a second batch quickly.

45 grams (about 3) poblano chilies, stemmed

30 grams (about 2) jalapeño chilies, stemmed

50 grams (about 1 head) garlic, cut in half

225 grams (about 1 medium) Spanish onion, cut into rings

Olive oil

85 grams (about 1 bunch) cilantro, whole, with stems

1 cup distilled white vinegar

1 cup apple cider vinegar

1. Position your Baking Steel Griddle on the stovetop. Preheat on medium-high for 10 to 15 minutes; you're looking for a surface temperature of 300 to 325°F.

2. Coat the poblanos, jalapeños, garlic, and onion slices with olive oil, then scatter them on top of the griddle and cook, stirring occasionally. Once softened and light brown but not charred, remove the vegetables from your griddle. Squeeze the garlic out of its paper, then transfer the entire mixture to a food processor or blender.

3. Pulse briefly just to get the puree started, then add in the cilantro, vinegars, and ¼ cup water. Puree until smooth. Season with salt. Adjust with more vinegar or water (a splash or two if the sauce seems too thick) to taste. Store leftovers in an airtight container in the refrigerator for up to 1 week.

Baking Steel on the Grill

Do you consider yourself a grill master? If so, this technique is bound to be a new feather in your cap; you can put your Baking Steel or Baking Steel Griddle right on top of your charcoal grill and cook directly on top of it.

The steel surface allows you to channel the heat from your grill, and it also prevents food from slipping between the grates.

1. Light the charcoal as usual, or fire up your gas grill.

2. Place the Baking Steel Griddle or Baking Steel on top of your grill.

3. Let the grill heat for 15 to 20 minutes; monitor the temperature using an instant-read thermometer.

4. Once the griddle is preheated to the temperature range for the item you're cooking, go for it with any of the recipes in this chapter.

When you're done cooking, be sure to leave ample time for the griddle to cool down before removing it from the grill surface.

SPATCHCOCKED CHICKEN

While it's become all the rage in recent years as a method for cooking Thanksgiving turkey, the art of spatchcocking is nothing new. To spatchcock poultry, or butterfly it, you remove the backbone, allowing it to be opened out and flattened. Think of it like butterflying a single piece of meat (page 199), but done to the whole bird. This technique reduces the cooking time significantly and allows the whole bird to be cooked in different ways, such as on a Baking Steel.

In this case, think of the Baking Steel as a heat sink that will regulate your oven temperature. The spatchcocked chicken is splayed out on a sheet tray and baked on top of the Baking Steel, which blasts heat right up into the sheet tray, cooking the chicken faster and better.

MAKES 2 TO 4 SERVINGS

1 whole chicken, 3 to 4 pounds

Olive oil

Fine sea salt and pepper

1. Position a rack in the middle of your oven and place the Baking Steel on top. Preheat oven to 425°F for 45 to 60 minutes.

2. Remove the liver and any chicken giblets, then place the chicken on a cutting board, breast-side down. Remove any excess fat.

3. To remove the backbone, run a finger along the back of the chicken to identify the bone and the soft outer side of the rib cage. This will show you where to cut.

4. Place the tip of a large sharp knife vertically to one side of the spine, insert it, and press down firmly. Bring the rest of the knife down along one side of the spine in one movement to cut all the way through. Alternatively, you can cut alongside the spine with sharp kitchen shears.

5. Repeat the technique on the other side of the spine, then remove the bone. The chicken can now be spread open; if desired, you can remove the wing tips with a sharp chef's knife.

6. Oil your chicken, and season it liberally with salt and pepper.

7. Place the chicken on a sheet tray and place the sheet tray on top of the preheated griddle. Cook for 20 to 25 minutes, or until the chicken attains an internal temperature of 165°F.

8. Remove from the oven and let cool on the sheet for several minutes before serving. Store well-wrapped leftovers in the refrigerator for up to 3 days.

PERFECT STEAK

I'll tell you one of the best advertisements for the Baking Steel: a perfectly seared steak. Several months ago, we incorporated a mini-version of the Baking Steel into our pizza classes. During the second half of the class, we would take a break from pizza to explore some of the Baking Steel's other capabilities.

You simply heat the griddle to the screaming-hot point, sear the steak for two to three minutes on either side, let the meat rest briefly, and serve. As soon as people taste it, there's a commotion and everyone asks: "How'd you do that?"

People are blown away by the versatility, but that's just the magic of the Baking Steel. When heated over the stovetop, the steel can attain high temperatures that begin to sear the meat practically the moment it hits the surface, creating a delicious crust.

While this recipe is tailored to my favorite cut, it can be used with any cut; simply adjust the cook time up or down depending on the size and thickness of the meat.

MAKES 1 STEAK

1 steak, approximately 1 inch thick
(I like a dry-aged New York strip steak)

Fine sea salt and pepper

1. Position your Baking Steel Griddle on the stovetop. Preheat on high heat for 10 to 15 minutes, aiming for a temperature range of 450 to 500°F. To test the surface, sprinkle a few drops of water on top; they should dance rapidly across the hot surface, evaporating in moments.

2. Let the steak rest at room temperature for 10 to 15 minutes. Pat the steak dry with paper towels and season generously on both sides with salt and pepper.

3. Using tongs, place the steak on the Baking Steel Griddle. It's going to sizzle and will shortly smoke, so be sure to throw that overhead vent on. Cook on the first side for 2 to 3 minutes, then flip and repeat on the second side. You're looking for an internal temperature of 145°F for medium steak; for medium-rare, stop at 140°F; for well done, take it to 150°F.

4. After the second side is done, remove with tongs and let rest for 10 minutes; this will help ensure that your meat is flavorful and moist.

5. Slice and serve.

ULTRA-SMASHED CHEESEBURGERS

I'm going to make a bold statement: This is simply the best burger you will ever make at home.

If you've somehow remained unaware of the smash-burger trend, it works like this: You start by forming your beef into a meatball. Then you put it on a hot surface and smash it like you mean it. This creates an inimitable sear on the bottom of the meat, sealing in all the flavor, and allows the meat to almost caramelize. It makes for a truly smashing (couldn't resist) burger experience.

In this recipe, culinary genius Kenji López-Alt takes the trend one step further and delivers a double-decker patty with gooey cheese sandwiched between the meat. It's truly last-meal-worthy.

MAKES 1 BURGER

1 soft hamburger bun, split, buttered and toasted (page 171)

Toppings: shredded lettuce, raw onions, sliced tomatoes, sliced pickles, Special Sauce (page 101)

120 grams (4 ounces) freshly ground beef chuck, divided into two 60-gram (2-ounce) balls

Salt and pepper

50 grams (1 slice) good melting cheese, such as American

1. Prepare your bun by laying toppings on the bottom half of the bun. Have it nearby and ready for when your burger is cooked.

2. Position your Baking Steel on the stovetop. Preheat on high heat for 10 to 15 minutes; you're looking for a surface temperature of 400 to 425°F. To test the surface, sprinkle a few drops of water on it; they should dance rapidly across the hot surface, evaporating in moments.

3. Place the balls of beef on the griddle and use a stiff metal spatula to smash them down; use a second spatula to add targeted pressure. Smashed patties should be slightly wider than the burger bun.

4. Season generously with salt and pepper and allow to cook until the bottom is well browned and the top is beginning to turn pale pink/gray in spots, about 45 seconds. Using a bench scraper or the back of a metal spatula, carefully scrape the burger patties from the surface, making sure to get all the tasty browned bits.

5. Flip patties and immediately place a slice of cheese over one patty, then stack the second patty directly on top. Remove from griddle and transfer to waiting bun. Serve immediately.

Sushi on Baking Steel

Everyone loves sushi (or at least, everyone should). Sushi really is an art form, learned only through observing, practicing, and repeating. It's not just sticky rice rolled up with some fish and vegetables.

While the Baking Steel isn't going to turn you into an expert sushi maker, it can make serving sushi much easier.

You see, while the Baking Steel is most famous for its even heating, it can also provide an even, steady cool temperature. This means that it's perfect for serving chilled food such as sushi.

Simply place your Baking Steel or Baking Steel Griddle in the freezer for about twenty minutes; now it's the ideal serving vessel for sushi. It's perfect for keeping sushi from overheating when you're entertaining on hot summer days.

BEEF SATAY

My mother raised me right; when I get invited to a party, I never show up empty-handed. These skewers are the perfect offering: a simple savory appetizer that will feed (and please) a crowd. Best of all, provided you've taken a few minutes to prep a marinade in advance, they cook extremely quickly.

The crisp sear and rich flavor on these steak skewers, thanks to the Baking Steel Griddle, make them taste fancy and decidedly chef-caliber. You can scale the recipe up if you'd like, because once you show up with these griddled wonders, you're going to get invited to a lot more parties.

MAKES 8 APPETIZER-SIZE SKEWERS

225 grams (8 ounces) flank steak

¼ cup soy sauce

2 tablespoons orange juice

5 grams (1 nub) fresh ginger, finely diced

5 grams (1 clove) garlic, finely diced

10 grams (about 2) scallion whites, finely diced (from the greens used for the chimichurri sauce)

110 grams (4½ cups) Griddled Scallion Chimichurri (recipe follows)

Special equipment

8 bamboo skewers, each about 6 inches long

1. Slice the flank steak across the grain into 8 long, thin strips. Try to make them as similar in size as possible. Skewer them on the bamboo sticks.

2. In a medium bowl, whisk together the soy sauce, orange juice, ginger, garlic, and scallions until combined.

3. Put the skewered steak into a gallon plastic bag, pour the marinade in, and seal the bag tightly. Allow the steak to marinate for 3 to 4 hours in the fridge.

4. When your skewers have marinated, position your Baking Steel on the stovetop. Preheat on medium-high for 10 to 15 minutes; you're looking for a temperature of 375 to 400°F. To test the surface, sprinkle a few drops of water on it; they should dance across the hot steel.

5. Sear the beef for about 15 seconds per side, looking for a pleasing char on both sides. Once cooked, transfer to a serving platter.

6. Garnish with Griddled Scallion Chimichurri and serve immediately.

CONT.

GRIDDLED SCALLION CHIMICHURRI

It's hard to overstate the addictive qualities of chimichurri sauce. Rumor has it that the sauce came about when Basque settlers hit Argentina in the late 1800s. Culinary fusion occurred, and the term *chimichurri* is said to be derived from the Basque word *tximitxurri*, loosely translated as "a mixture of several things in no particular order." Regardless of where the funny name comes from, this is undoubtedly a sauce that tastes great on everything.

¾ cup olive oil

90 grams (1 bunch) scallions, sliced

Fine sea salt and pepper

5 grams (1 clove) garlic, diced

85 grams (approximately 2 ounces, or 1 bunch) cilantro

85 grams (approximately 2 ounces, or 1 bunch) parsley

25 grams (about 2 tablespoons) crushed red pepper flakes

1 cup apple cider vinegar

1. Place your Baking Steel on top of your stove. Heat on medium for 10 to 15 minutes; you're looking for a temperature of 325 to 350°F. To test the surface, sprinkle a few drops of water on it; they should dance across the hot steel.

2. In a small bowl, combine 3 tablespoons of the olive oil, the scallions, and salt and pepper to taste. Carefully scatter the mixture on the hot griddle.

3. Cook, shifting the mixture around using a spatula, until the scallions begin to soften, gain color, and wilt slightly. This will take 4 to 5 minutes. Remove using heatproof tongs and transfer to a blender.

4. Add the remaining ingredients (except the olive oil) to the blender and blend until smooth. Drizzle in the remaining olive oil; adjust for consistency and flavor. Store in an airtight container in the fridge for up to 3 weeks.

SAVORY GALETTE

There's a lot to love about savory vegetable galettes. They're easy to make, hearty to eat, and can be made using whatever seasonal produce you can get your hands on. Less lovable? These free-form savory tarts, with their moist ingredients, tend to suffer from a serious case of soggy crust.

The Baking Steel can help you avoid the abomination that is the sad, waterlogged crust. The even heat dispersion of the steel allows for the fillings to cook faster, meaning that when the top and bottom of the galette are crisped to perfection, the fillings are fully set, resulting in a soft—but not soggy—interior.

MAKES ONE 9-INCH TART

For the crust

300 grams (2½ cups) all-purpose flour

5 grams (1 teaspoon) fine sea salt

16 tablespoons unsalted butter, very cold, cut into cubes

½ cup water, ice cold

For the filling

150 grams (1 bunch) tatsoi root, cut and washed (you can substitute fresh spinach or baby bok choy)

120 grams (1 small) Vidalia onion, julienned on a mandoline or very thinly sliced

4 grams (2 cloves) garlic, shaved thin

2 tablespoons olive oil

Fine sea salt and pepper

½ cup No-Cook Tomato Sauce (page 48)

113 grams (4 ounces) feta, crumbled

1 large egg beaten with 1 teaspoon water

Fresh oregano leaves

1. Make the crust. Using a food processor, pulse the flour and salt for a few seconds to combine. Next, add the cold butter cubes, a few at a time. Pulse until the largest crumbs are the size of peas. Slowly add the cold water and pulse until the mixture just comes together. Remove and knead the mixture until it forms a loose dough. Divide in half and form disks; cover with plastic wrap and place in the refrigerator for at least an hour or until needed (see note opposite).

2. Position your Baking Steel on a rack in the middle of your oven. Preheat the oven to 350°F for 45 to 60 minutes.

3. Make the filling. On either a Baking Steel Griddle or in a skillet set over medium heat, quickly sauté the tatsoi, onions, and garlic in olive oil and season with salt and pepper. Cook just until softened, 2 to 3 minutes. Remove from heat, transfer to a bowl, and briefly chill in the refrigerator.

4. Meanwhile, roll out the galette dough on parchment paper into a circle about 12 inches in diameter and about ¼ inch thick.

5. Spread tomato sauce in the circle, leaving about 3 inches of space around the perimeter.

6. Spoon the vegetable mix on top of the tomato sauce. Sprinkle the feta evenly on top.

7. Fold the edges of the crust over the filling, but leave the center exposed (the fold-over should extend in about 2 inches).

8. Brush the top of the crust with your egg wash; sprinkle oregano leaves on top.

9. Either place your parchment on a sheet tray and put it on your Baking Steel or use a pizza peel to launch the parchment sheet directly onto your steel. Bake for about 18 to 20 minutes, rotating after 10 minutes, until golden brown. Remove and transfer to a wire rack to cool slightly before serving. Serve warm. Store well-wrapped leftovers in the refrigerator for up to 2 days.

NOTE: The pie dough featured in this recipe yields two portions. This is a great thing for two reasons. First, once you make this galette, you'll absolutely want to make it again. You can also use the leftover dough to make the Apple Hand Pies (page 230). If you want to use your extra dough to make dessert, consider adding up to 5 teaspoons of granulated sugar to the flour-and-salt mixture before incorporating the butter. The slightly sweetened dough will work well for this galette too. This dough can be made in advance and refrigerated up to 3 days or frozen for 1 month.

MEXICAN STREET-STYLE CORN

It wouldn't be summer without corn on the cob. But if you want to give your kernels a kick, take a cue from South of the Border street-food vendors and make Mexican-style corn (also called *elotes*). After grilling your corn, you'll season it with cheese, chili powder, and cilantro for a tasty cob that's spicy, sweet, and creamy—everything summer food should be.

The Baking Steel helps you get that perfectly charred grill effect right on your stovetop. It cooks the corn evenly so you don't end up with dried-out kernels. Juicy corn, robust spices: these ears are a delicious study in flavor and texture contrasts.

MAKES 8 HALF-COBS

8 tablespoons unsalted butter, melted

30 grams (1 tablespoon) dark chili powder

4 ears of corn, each one cut in half

Fine sea salt and pepper

125 grams (4 ounces) cotija cheese, grated

60 grams (2 ounces) cilantro, chopped

Special equipment

8 wooden skewers

1. Position your Baking Steel Griddle on the stovetop. Preheat on medium-high for 10 to 15 minutes; you're looking for a surface temperature of 350 to 375°F. To test the surface, sprinkle a few drops of water on it; they should dance across the hot steel.

2. In a medium bowl, combine the melted butter and chili powder. Brush the corn with this mixture, reserving a little bit to top off the corn post-grilling, and place it on the Baking Steel.

3. Cook the corn, turning every so often so that you get a good color on all sides. This can take anywhere from 10 to 20 minutes.

4. Remove corn, brush with more butter and chili powder, and sprinkle with salt and pepper. Sprinkle with cheese, garnish with cilantro, and push the cobs onto skewers for easy party-time handling. Serve immediately.

DIY Baking Steel Hot Surface with Sterno

Tailgaters, campers, and outdoor enthusiasts, rejoice! A grill isn't the only way you can bring your Baking Steel outside. With minimal investment and setup, you can transform any outdoor place into your personal kitchen by using Sterno to heat your Baking Steel. Here's how you do it.

1. Start by choosing a place where your Baking Steel can remain undisturbed while it heats and cools, avoiding areas that are sensitive to heat (not on top of the disposable tablecloth, please).

2. Set up bricks in a U shape and place the Baking Steel on top.

3. Place 4 to 5 cans of Sterno, evenly spaced, below the steel; put them on the ground or on a baking sheet, something that can resist heat. The Sternos heat the Baking Steel, and in 30 minutes it's good and hot. Now you can make burgers, steak, or whatever suits your outdoor-entertaining needs.

DESSERT

ICE CREAM IN MINUTES

It's hard to resist the sweet siren call of ice cream. Kids, adults, and foodies of all ages will love this unique recipe, which combines everyone's favorite dessert with a little mad science.

Forget about an ice cream maker; we're going to use dry ice, which has the power to turn your Baking Steel into a −38°F ice block and the ideal ice cream canvas. Try doing that with your pizza stone or a baking sheet!

Chill your Baking Steel with dry ice, then, once you make your rich custard base, transfer it to the steel. Working with bench scrapers, you'll knead the custard into some of the richest, creamiest ice cream you've ever had the pleasure of putting in your mouth.

MAKES 4 SERVINGS

4 egg yolks

50 grams (¼ cup) sugar

2 grams (about ½ teaspoon) fine sea salt

½ vanilla bean, split and scraped, pod reserved

1 cup whole milk

1 cup heavy cream

Special equipment

3 pounds dry ice pellets (see note on page 224)

1. Prepare an ice-water bath by filling your sink (or a large bowl) with ice and cold water. It should be large enough to allow your ice cream mixing bowl to rest inside it.

2. Beat the yolks, sugar, and salt by hand with a whisk until pale yellow and thick, about 5 minutes.

3. Meanwhile, scrape the vanilla seeds into a medium saucepan and add the pod, milk, and cream. Bring the mixture to a hard simmer—that is, when bubbles have formed but are not in rolling motion—then remove from heat.

4. Pour about half of the hot milk mixture into the yolk mixture, whisking constantly while pouring to discourage the eggs from scrambling.

5. Once thoroughly combined, pour the yolk-milk mixture back into the saucepan with the remaining milk mixture. Cook over medium-low heat, stirring constantly with a wooden spoon, until mixture is thick enough to coat the back of the spoon and hold a line drawn by your finger, about 4 to 6 minutes.

CONT.

6. Strain the mixture through a fine sieve into a bowl to remove any bits of egg that have formed. Place the bowl in the ice-water bath. Stir every few minutes until it is thoroughly chilled.

7. Being careful not to allow the dry ice to touch your skin, use oven mitts to pour the dry ice pellets onto a rimmed cookie sheet. Place the Baking Steel Griddle on top of the dry ice and wait 5 minutes. Your griddle is going to get very cold very fast (we're talking –25 to –50°F), so do not touch it directly!

8. Pour your chilled crème anglaise (that's the ice cream base) on top of the chilled griddle and work rapidly with a bench scraper to move the liquid around until it has chilled enough to set. The mixture will freeze very quickly, so work confidently and fast!

9. This ice cream can be served immediately; store leftovers in the freezer in an airtight container.

NOTE: Dry ice is more readily available than you might think. If you Google *dry ice* and the city you live in, chances are you'll come up with a myriad of results. But actually, my best tip is to look at your local supermarket. Many larger supermarkets have dry ice available for purchase. At more than 100 degrees below zero, dry ice is cold enough to burn your skin, so be sure to handle it with an oven mitt or gloves.

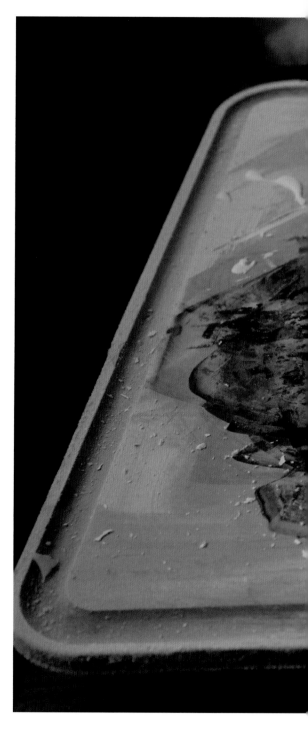

Ice Cream Entertaining with Baking Steel

I scream, you scream, we all scream for ice cream, right? Well, I have a son with both nut and egg allergies, so enjoying ice cream at a parlor can sometimes be a bit of a challenge. Wanting him to try flavors beyond basic vanilla, I was inspired to use the Baking Steel to create custom mix-in ice cream for him. If you want to put on a show for your guests and delight kids, I suggest you do the same. Here's how.

1. Place your clean Baking Steel inside the freezer for several hours or overnight.

2. With your steel safely tucked away, take a quick trip to the grocer for your favorite ice cream (homemade or store-bought is fine) and mix-in ingredients. Remember, the sky's the limit on this one; mix-ins are your personal preference, so go crazy! I love chocolate chip mint, so I bought some vanilla ice cream, fresh mint, and chocolate chunks.

3. Once your steel is thoroughly chilled, you've got your cold plate and ice cream palette. Remove the steel from the freezer and place it on the counter with a towel underneath to prevent slippage.

4. Scoop a generous amount of ice cream on top of the steel and spread it using a bench scraper. Scatter your mix-ins on top, and then knead the mixture using your bench scraper until evenly distributed. Voilà! Gourmet mixed ice cream, right in your own home!

PANTRY COOKIES

Ready to shake up your cookie-making technique? Ditch the baking sheet: you can bake cookies right on top of a parchment-lined Baking Steel, with superior results. You've never seen the bottoms of cookies bake so perfectly: the sides and tops of the cookies are crunchy, with an irresistibly chewy interior. Plus, baking cookies on the steel shaves a few minutes off the baking time. These cookies, full of unusual mix-ins, are sweet-and-salty perfection.

MAKES 12 LARGE COOKIES

210 grams (1⅔ cups) all-purpose flour

5 grams (1 teaspoon) baking soda

10 grams (2 teaspoons) fine sea salt

16 tablespoons unsalted butter, softened

220 grams (1 cup) packed dark brown sugar

100 grams (½ cup) granulated sugar

2 large eggs

1 teaspoon vanilla extract

90 grams (1 cup) rolled oats

175 grams (1 cup) semisweet chocolate chips

175 grams (1 cup) peanut butter chips

45 grams (a handful) kettle-cooked potato chips

45 grams (a handful) mini–pretzel twists

1. Place your Baking Steel on the middle rack of your oven. Preheat oven to 350°F for 45 to 60 minutes.

2. In a large bowl, sift together the flour, baking soda, and salt. Set aside.

3. In a stand mixer fitted with the paddle attachment, cream the butter and sugars until fluffy and light, 2 to 3 minutes on medium-high.

4. Add eggs one at a time and beat until combined. Stir in the vanilla extract.

5. Add the flour mixture to the wet mixture in 2 batches and mix on low until just incorporated.

6. Fold in the oats, chocolate and peanut butter chips, potato chips, and pretzels. Chill the dough, right in the mixing bowl, for 30 minutes in the refrigerator. By the time your dough has chilled, the Baking Steel should be perfectly heated.

7. Place 4-ounce cookie dough balls, leaving 2 inches of space between them for the cookies to spread, on top of a sheet of parchment paper.

8. Using a pizza peel, launch the parchment paper onto the hot Baking Steel. Bake for 12 to 14 minutes, rotating halfway through baking, until golden brown. Remove using the peel and transfer the sheet of parchment to a wire rack to allow the cookies to cool. Store in an airtight container for up to 5 days or freeze for up to 1 month.

APPLE HAND PIES

I'm sorry, are you still using a plate to eat your pie? Get with the Instagram trend, ditch the plate, and bake your pies as handheld units! So-called hand pies are just what they sound like: a generous, hearty slab of pie crust filled like a DIY Pop-Tart.

Cooking the pies on the Baking Steel on a parchment sheet ensures that you get a bottom crust that is crispy, never gummy. Filled with a classic apple-pie filling, these pies may not be traditional in form but they fit the bill in the flavor department.

MAKES 6 HAND PIES

For the pie crust

1 ball pie dough (from Savory Galette recipe, page 216; if making the dough just for hand pies, see note about sweetening your dough)

1 large egg, beaten with 1 teaspoon water

For the apple filling

4 or 5 medium McIntosh apples, peeled and chopped

100 grams (4 tablespoons) brown sugar

5 grams (2 teaspoons) ground cinnamon

½ cup orange juice

1 teaspoon vanilla extract

4 tablespoons unsalted butter

36 grams (3 tablespoons) cornstarch

3 tablespoons water, cold

1. Make the crust in advance using the dough recipe from page 216. If desired, stir in up to 5 teaspoons of granulated sugar with the flour and salt. This is optional, but the sugar can help the crust pair nicely with the sweetness of the filling.

2. Place your Baking Steel on the middle rack in your oven. Preheat oven to 400°F for 45 to 60 minutes.

3. Make the filling. In a large bowl, toss the chopped apples together with the brown sugar, cinnamon, orange juice, and vanilla and mix until the pieces are evenly coated.

4. In a large saucepan on medium heat, melt and brown the butter. Add the apple mixture and cook over medium heat, stirring occasionally, for 10 minutes.

5. Meanwhile, stir together the cornstarch and cold water until it forms a smooth slurry without any lumps. Add the cornstarch mixture to the apple mixture and stir until the liquid coats the back of a spoon.

6. Remove the mixture from the pan and pour it on a sheet tray to allow it to cool.

7. Assemble the pies: Roll out pie dough to about ⅛ inch thick. Cut out 12 equal-size circles, squares, or rectangles (one each for the top and bottom of each pie), roughly 3 inches in diameter.

8. Place 6 portions of dough on a piece of parchment paper; these are your pie bottoms.

9. Spoon the apple filling in the center of each piece. Brush the outer perimeter of the dough with a small amount of your egg wash; place the remaining dough portions on top. They will naturally have a domed shape. Press the edges together to form a seal and then crimp the crust all around by pressing down with the tines of a fork. Poke a hole in the top of each pie to allow the steam to escape while the pies bake.

10. Brush the surface of each pie with the remainder of your egg wash. Then either place your parchment on a sheet tray and put that on your Baking Steel or use a pizza peel to launch the parchment sheet directly onto your steel.

11. Bake for about 15 minutes or until the crust is browned to your liking; rotate halfway through baking. Remove and let cool on wire racks. Serve slightly warm. Store well-wrapped leftovers at room temperature for up to 2 days.

DORAYAKI

If you've never sampled the sweet Japanese snack dorayaki, you're in for a real treat. Picture a pancake. Next, picture it topped with a generous dollop of sweet filling—in this case, raspberry jam—with a second pancake on top of that.

Dora is Japanese for "gong"; while this likely refers to the round shape of the cakes, I like to think it's a shout-out to their resounding deliciousness. Once you've mastered the method of making these sweet, fluffy pancakes on the Baking Steel Griddle, you can experiment with different fillings. In Japan, it's customary to fill them with sweet red bean paste, but you can follow our lead and use jam or experiment with something else entirely—maybe even ice cream.

MAKES ABOUT 12 SANDWICHES

4 large eggs

150 grams (¾ cup) sugar

1 tablespoon honey

150 grams (1¼ cups) all-purpose flour, sifted

1 gram (¼ teaspoon) baking powder

2 teaspoons water, cold

Canola oil

325 grams (1 cup) raspberry jam

1. In a large bowl, whisk the eggs, sugar, and honey for about 2 minutes, making sure that everything is well combined. The mixture will be somewhat foamy.

2. Add the flour and baking powder to the bowl; whisk to combine, then let the bowl sit undisturbed for about 5 minutes.

3. Add the cold water and whisk briefly to combine. Transfer the bowl to the refrigerator; let it rest there for 10 to 15 minutes.

4. Meanwhile, position your Baking Steel or Baking Steel Griddle on the stovetop. Preheat on medium-low for 10 to 15 minutes; you're looking for a surface temperature of 200 to 250°F.

5. Oil the griddle lightly with canola oil; it should begin to bubble when it hits the surface. Immediately (and very carefully; the surface is hot) wipe it off using paper towels to leave the very thinnest layer of oil possible.

6. Pour about 2 to 3 tablespoons of batter on top of the heated Baking Steel Griddle to form each pancake, making a few at a time as space allows. After about 60 seconds, bubbles will begin to form; this is a good indication that it is time to flip.

7. Flip and cook for about 15 to 20 seconds on the second side.

8. Remove the pancakes and transfer them to a plate, then continue with the remaining batter.

9. To assemble, spread a generous tablespoon of jam on one pancake and place a similar-size pancake on top. Repeat with the rest of the pancakes. Serve immediately.

TEMPERED CHOCOLATE

To novice chocolatiers, tempering sounds scary and advanced, like something you probably need a pastry-chef certification to do properly. But it's just a matter of heating and cooling chocolate in a controlled way to improve its texture and durability. First, you melt the chocolate, then you rapidly cool it, in this case by pouring the melted chocolate on a room-temperature Baking Steel Griddle. This causes stable crystals of cocoa butter to form. When brought back up to a working temperature, these crystals create the perfect snap of a candy bar and the impeccably glossy, smooth texture of dipped candies. If you don't temper your chocolate, your confections are likely to form ugly white spots (termed *blooming*) a day or two after they've been dipped.

Tempering chocolate is simple using the Baking Steel Griddle; it provides the ideal surface to rapidly cool your heated chocolate. Make your countertop your own kitchen laboratory!

Note: Read this recipe entirely before you give it a try. Step 2 requires a little bit of finesse. Ideally, you start by holding your tools and having a friend slowly pour the chocolate onto the surface for you. If you're working solo, have the bench scraper in one hand as you pour so that you can shift the chocolate around immediately, reducing the chance of spilling it on your countertop. Once the chocolate is poured, grab the spatula with your other hand and work the two tools in tandem to spread the chocolate across the surface of the steel until it firms.

1 kilogram (35 ounces) dark chocolate

Fruit, cookies, or whatever you'd like to dip in the chocolate

1. Using a double boiler or a bowl set in a saucepan full of water, melt the chocolate. Monitor the temperature using a candy thermometer or instant-read thermometer; you want the chocolate to reach a temperature between 104 to 113°F (40 to 45°C). Remove from heat.

2. Moving quickly, pour two-thirds of the melted chocolate onto the room-temperature Baking Steel Griddle surface. Immediately begin to work the chocolate across the surface of the steel. I like to do this with a spatula in my dominant hand to move the chocolate and a bench scraper in my other hand to keep the mixture from spreading too far or going over the edges. Keep the chocolate moving until it becomes too firm to continue working.

3. Scrape the thickened chocolate off the griddle and back into the bowl with the remaining melted chocolate. Stir until incorporated. When you lift the chocolate with a spatula, it will spread in ribbons, and your chocolate now has a beautiful shine.

4. Congratulations—your chocolate is tempered! Now you're ready to coat truffles, dip fruit, decorate cakes, or do whatever your heart desires with it. To make it easier to work with, keep the chocolate in the top of a double boiler so that you can rewarm as needed.

ACKNOWLEDGMENTS

About four months after our Kickstarter campaign, I was contacted by my now literary agent, Alexandra Penfold. We weren't quite ready for a book project yet, but, Alexandra, you planted the seed of inspiration. There is no way this book would ever have happened without your persistence—thank you. And thank you for introducing me to Jessie Oleson Moore. Jessie, you turn words upside down and inside out. You are a pink, fluffy unicorn dancing on rainbows!

Fresh Chef Craig Hastings, you are an inspiration, my man! Your amazing chef skills helped make this book happen. You made it so much fun to create and test recipes. I truly appreciate everything you do. Thank you.

Thank you, Stoughton Steel! The Baking Steel has been a journey for us all. Thank you for your constructive criticism—your uncertainty pushed me to make this product succeed! A shout-out to my brother Eric for getting all of the Baking Steels manufactured and shipped on time, every single day.

To the *Wall Street Journal:* thank you for interviewing Nathan Myhrvold for the launch of his book *Modernist Cuisine.* I still consider the Baking Steel a ripple effect of my reading that article. I'll never forget those moments in my office...still feels like a dream. And thank you, Scott Heimendinger at Modernist Cuisine, for answering my e-mail when I began to develop the Baking Steel. You helped my dream come true.

To Michael and Nicky at Little, Brown and Co.: Thank you for all that you do. You guys are magic!

To Kenji López-Alt at Serious Eats: thanks for being a "food nerd" and loving the Baking Steel! You single-handedly put the Baking Steel on the map.

Thank you to all my friends, who continue to help me along this journey. There are too many of you to name.

Thank you to all our loyal and pizza-obsessed customers. I love all of your e-mails and support.

I'm grateful for the crowdsourcing site Kickstarter for helping to make dreams come true. And to all 482 Baking Steel backers, I'm eternally grateful.

Last, and most important, thank you to Leslie, Cooper, and Gus, for being there with me throughout this journey. None of this would have happened without you. You all "steel" my heart every day!—A.L.

A big, cheesy, pepperoni-on-top thank-you goes to my co-writer, Andris Lagsdin, for being an all-around fun collaborator and a true source of culinary inspiration and delight.

To the crew at Little, Brown and Company and to our agent, Alexandra Penfold: Thank you for helping make this book a reality! You are all superstars with great vision, talent, and attention to detail, and you're officially invited to any and every pizza party I ever have for the rest of my life.—J.M.

INDEX

Page numbers in *italic* refer to photographs.